Harvard Business Review

ON

KNOWLEDGE MANAGEMENT

THE HARVARD BUSINESS REVIEW PAPERBACK SERIES

The series is designed to bring today's managers and professionals the fundamental information they need to stay competitive in a fast-moving world. From the preeminent thinkers whose work has defined an entire field to the rising stars who will redefine the way we think about business, here are the leading minds and landmark ideas that have established the *Harvard Business Review* as required reading for ambitious businesspeople in organizations around the globe.

Other books in the series:

Harvard Business Review on Change

Harvard Business Review on Leadership

Harvard Business Review on Measuring Corporate Performance

Harvard Business Review on Strategies for Growth

Harvard Business Review

ON

KNOWLEDGE MANAGEMENT

A HARVARD BUSINESS REVIEW PAPERBACK

The paper used in this publication meets the requirements of the American National Standard for Permanence of Paper for Printed Library Materials Z39.49-1984.

Contents

Harvard Business Review

ON

KNOWLEDGE MANAGEMENT

The Coming of the
New Organization

PETER F. DRUCKER

Executive Summary

TWENTY YEARS FROM NOW, the typical large business
will have half the levels of management and one-third
the managers of its counterpart today. Work will be
done by specialists brought together in task forces that
cut across traditional departments. Coordination and
control will depend largely on employees' willingness to
discipline themselves.

Behind these changes lies information technology.
Computers communicate faster and better than layers of
middle management. They also demand knowledgeable users who can transform their data into information.

Clues to what the new, information-based organizations will require come from other knowledge-based enti-
ties like hospitals and symphony orchestras. First, a
"score"—a set of clear, simple objectives that translate
into particular actions. Second, a structure in which

1

everyone takes information responsibility by asking:
Who depends on me for what information? On whom
do I depend?

Information-based organizations pose their own special management problems as well: motivating and rewarding specialists; creating a vision that can unify an organization of specialists; devising a management structure that works with task forces; and ensuring the supply, preparation, and testing of top management people.

Solving these problems is the management challenge for the rest of the century.

THE TYPICAL LARGE BUSINESS 20 years hence will have fewer than half the levels of management of its counterpart today, and no more than a third the managers. In its structure, and in its management problems and concerns, it will bear little resemblance to the typical manufacturing company, circa 1950, which our textbooks still consider the norm. Instead it is far more likely to resemble organizations that neither the practicing manager nor the management scholar pays much attention to today: the hospital, the university, the symphony orchestra. For like them, the typical business will be knowledge-based, an organization composed largely of specialists who direct and discipline their own performance through organized feedback from colleagues, customers, and headquarters. For this reason, it will be what I call an information-based organization.

Businesses, especially large ones, have little choice but to become information-based. Demographics, for one, demands the shift. The center of gravity in employment is moving fast from manual and clerical workers to knowledge workers who resist the command-and-control model that business took from the military 100 years ago. Economics also dictates change, especially the need for large businesses to innovate and to be entrepreneurs. But above all, information technology demands the shift.

The large business 20 years hence is more likely to resemble a hospital or a symphony than a typical manufacturing company.

Advanced data-processing technology isn't necessary to create an information-based organization, of course. As we shall see, the British built just such an organization in India when "information technology" meant the quill pen, and barefoot runners were the "telecommunications" systems. But as advanced technology becomes more and more prevalent, we have to engage in analysis and diagnosis—that is, in "information"—even more intensively or risk being swamped by the data we generate.

So far most computer users still use the new technology only to do faster what they have always done before, crunch conventional numbers. But as soon as a company takes the first tentative steps from data to information, its decision processes, management structure, and even the way its work gets done begin to be transformed. In fact, this is already happening, quite fast, in a number of companies throughout the world.

WE CAN READILY SEE the first step in this transformation process when we consider the impact of computer technology on capital-investment decisions.

We have known for a long time that there is no one right way to analyze a proposed capital investment. To understand it we need at least six analyses: the expected rate of return; the payout period and the investment's expected productive life; the discounted present value of all returns through the productive lifetime of the investment; the risk in not making the investment or deferring it; the cost and risk in case of failure; and finally, the opportunity cost. Every accounting student is taught these concepts. But before the advent of data-processing capacity, the actual analyses would have taken man-years of clerical toil to complete. Now anyone with a spreadsheet should be able to do them in a few hours.

The availability of this information transforms the capital-investment analysis from opinion into diagnosis, that is, into the rational weighing of alternative assumptions. Then the information transforms the capital-investment decision from an opportunistic, financial decision governed by the numbers into a business decision based on the probability of alternative strategic assumptions. So the decision both presupposes a business strategy and challenges that strategy and its assumptions. What was once a budget exercise becomes an analysis of policy.

The second area that is affected when a company focuses its data-processing capacity on producing information is its organization structure. Almost immediately, it becomes clear that both the number of management levels and the number of managers can be sharply cut. The reason is straightforward: it turns out that whole layers of man-

Information transforms a budget exercise into an analysis of policy.

agement neither make decisions nor lead. Instead, their
main, if not their only, function is to serve as "relays"—
human boosters for the faint, unfocused signals
that pass for communication in the traditional pre-
information organization.

One of America's largest defense contractors made
this discovery when it asked what information its top
corporate and operating managers needed to do their
jobs. Where did it come from? What form was it in?
How did it flow? The search for answers soon revealed
that whole layers of management—perhaps as many as 6
out of a total of 14—existed only because these questions had not been asked before. The company had had
data galore. But it had always used its copious data for
control rather than for information.

Information is data endowed with relevance and purpose. Converting data into information thus requires
knowledge. And knowledge, by definition, is specialized.
(In fact, truly knowledgeable people tend toward over-
specialization, whatever their field, precisely because
there is always so much more to know.)

The information-based organization requires far
more specialists overall than the command-and-control
companies we are accustomed to. Moreover, the specialists are found in operations, not at corporate headquarters. Indeed, the operating organization tends to become
an organization of specialists of all kinds.

Information-based organizations need central operating work such as legal counsel, public relations, and
labor relations as much as ever. But the need for service
staffs—that is, for people without operating responsibilities who only advise, counsel, or coordinate—shrinks
drastically. In its *central* management, the information-
based organization needs few, if any, specialists.

Because of its flatter structure, the large, information-based organization will more closely resemble the businesses of a century ago

Traditional departments than today's big companies.
won't be where the work Back then, however, all the
gets done. knowledge, such as it was, lay with the very top people. The rest were helpers or hands, who mostly did the same work and did as they were told. In the information-based organization, the knowledge will be primarily at the bottom, in the minds of the specialists who do different work and direct themselves. So today's typical organization in which knowledge tends to be concentrated in service staffs, perched rather insecurely between top management and the operating people, will likely be labeled a phase, an attempt to infuse knowledge from the top rather than obtain information from below.

Finally, a good deal of work will be done differently in the information-based organization. Traditional departments will serve as guardians of standards, as centers for training and the assignment of specialists; they won't be where the work gets done. That will happen largely in task-focused teams.

This change is already under way in what used to be the most clearly defined of all departments—research. In pharmaceuticals, in telecommunications, in papermaking, the traditional *sequence* of research, development, manufacturing, and marketing is being replaced by synchrony: specialists from all these functions work together as a team, from the inception of research to a product's establishment in the market.

How task forces will develop to tackle other business opportunities and problems remains to be seen. I suspect, however, that the need for a task force, its assignment, its composition, and its leadership will have to be decided on case by case. So the organization that will be developed will go beyond the matrix and may indeed be quite different from it. One thing is clear, though: it will require greater self-discipline and even greater emphasis on individual responsibility for relationships and for communications.

T O SAY THAT INFORMATION TECHNOLOGY is transforming business enterprises is simple. What this transformation will require of companies and top managements is much harder to decipher. That is why I find it helpful to look for clues in other kinds of information-based organizations, such as the hospital, the symphony orchestra, and the British administration in India.

A fair-sized hospital of about 400 beds will have a staff of several hundred physicians and 1,200 to 1,500 paramedics divided among some 60 medical and paramedical specialties. Each specialty has its own knowledge, its own training, its own language. In each specialty, especially the paramedical ones like the clinical lab and physical therapy, there is a head person who is a working specialist rather than a full-time manager. The head of each specialty reports directly to the top, and there is little middle management. A good deal of the work is done in ad hoc teams as required by an individual patient's diagnosis and condition.

The best example of a large and successful information-based organization had no middle management at all.

A large symphony orchestra is even more instructive, since for some works there may be a few hundred musicians on stage playing together. According to

organization theory then, there should be several group
vice president conductors and perhaps a half-dozen division VP conductors. But that's not how it works. There is
only the conductor-CEO—and every one of the musicians
plays directly to that person without an intermediary.
And each is a high-grade specialist, indeed an artist.

But the best example of a large and successful
information-based organization, and one without any
middle management at all, is the British civil administration in India.[1]

The British ran the Indian subcontinent for 200 years,
from the middle of the eighteenth century through
World War II, without making any fundamental changes
in organization structure or administrative policy. The
Indian civil service never had more than 1,000 members
to administer the vast and densely populated subcontinent—a tiny fraction (at most 1%) of the legions of Con-
fucian mandarins and palace eunuchs employed next
door to administer a not-much-more populous China.
Most of the Britishers were quite young; a 30-year-old
was a survivor, especially in the early years. Most lived
alone in isolated outposts with the nearest countryman
a day or two of travel away, and for the first hundred
years there was no telegraph or railroad.

The organization structure was totally flat. Each district officer reported directly to the "Coo," the provincial
political secretary. And since there were nine provinces,
each political secretary had at least 100 people reporting
directly to him, many times what the doctrine of the
span of control would allow. Nevertheless, the system
worked remarkably well, in large part because it was
designed to ensure that each of its members had the
information he needed to do his job.

Each month the district officer spent a whole day

writing a full report to the political secretary in the provincial capital. He discussed each of his principal tasks—there were only four, each clearly delineated. He put down in detail what he had expected would happen with respect to each of them, what actually did happen, and why, if there was a discrepancy, the two differed. Then he wrote down what he expected would happen in the ensuing month with respect to each key task and what he was going to do about it, asked questions about policy, and commented on long-term opportunities, threats, and needs. In turn, the political secretary "minuted" every one of those reports—that is, he wrote back a full comment.

O N THE BASIS OF THESE EXAMPLES, what can we say about the requirements of the information-based organization? And what are its management problems likely to be? Let's look first at the requirements. Several hundred musicians and their CEO, the conductor, can play together because they all have the same score. It tells both flutist and timpanist what to play and when. And it tells the conductor what to expect from each and when. Similarly, all the specialists in the hospital share a common mission: the care and cure of the sick. The diagnosis is their "score"; it dictates specific action for the X-ray lab, the dietitian, the physical therapist, and the rest of the medical team.

Information-based organizations, in other words, require clear, simple, common objectives that translate into particular actions. At the same time, however, as these examples indicate, information-based organizations also need concentration on one objective or, at most, on a few.

Because the "players" in an information-based organization are specialists, they cannot be told how to do their work. There are probably few orchestra conductors who could coax even one note out of a French horn, let alone show the horn player how to do it. But the conductor can focus the horn player's skill and knowledge on the musicians' joint performance. And this focus is what the leaders of an information-based business must be able to achieve.

Yet a business has no "score" to play by except the score it writes as it plays. And whereas neither a first-rate performance of a symphony nor a miserable one will change what the composer wrote, the performance of a business continually creates new and different scores against which its performance is assessed. So an information-based business must be structured around goals that clearly state management's performance expectations for the enterprise and for each part and specialist and around organized feedback that compares results with these performance expectations so that every member can exercise self-control.

The other requirement of an information-based organization is that everyone take information responsibility. The bassoonist in the orchestra does so every time she plays a note. Doctors and paramedics work with an elaborate system of reports and an information center, the nurse's station on the patient's floor. The district officer in India acted on this responsibility every time he filed a report.

Who depends on me for information? And on whom do I depend?

The key to such a system is that everyone asks: Who in this organization depends on me for what information? And on whom, in turn, do I depend? Each person's list will always include superiors and subordinates. But the most important names on it will be those of colleagues, people with whom one's primary relationship is coordination. The relationship of the internist, the surgeon, and the anesthesiologist is one example. But the relationship of a biochemist, a pharmacologist, the medical director in charge of clinical testing, and a marketing specialist in a pharmaceutical company is no different. It, too, requires each party to take the fullest information responsibility.

Information responsibility to others is increasingly understood, especially in middle-sized companies. But information responsibility to oneself is still largely neglected. That is, everyone in an organization should constantly be thinking through what information he or she needs to do the job and to make a contribution.

This may well be the most radical break with the way even the most highly computerized businesses are still being run today. There, people either assume the more data, the more information—which was a perfectly valid assumption yesterday when data were scarce, but leads to data overload and information blackout now that they are plentiful. Or they believe that information specialists know what data executives and professionals need in order to have information. But information specialists are tool makers. They can tell us what tool to use to hammer upholstery nails into a chair. We need to decide whether we should be upholstering a chair at all.

To remain competitive—maybe even to survive—businesses will have to convert themselves into organizations of knowledgeable specialists.

Executives and professional specialists need to think through what information is for them, what data they need: first, to know what they are doing; then, to be able to decide what they should be doing; and finally, to appraise how well they are doing. Until this happens MIS departments are likely to remain cost centers rather than become the result centers they could be.

M OST LARGE BUSINESSES have little in common with the examples we have been looking at. Yet to remain competitive—maybe even to survive—they will have to convert themselves into information-based organizations, and fairly quickly. They will have to change old habits and acquire new ones. And the more successful a company has been, the more difficult and painful this process is apt to be. It will threaten the jobs, status, and opportunities of a good many people in the organization, especially the long-serving, middle-aged people in middle management who tend to be the least mobile and to feel most secure in their work, their positions, their relationships, and their behavior.

The information-based organization will also pose its own special management problems. I see as particularly critical:

1. Developing rewards, recognition, and career opportunities for specialists.

2. Creating unified vision in an organization of specialists.

3. Devising the management structure for an organization of task forces.

4. Ensuring the supply, preparation, and testing of top management people.

Bassoonists presumably neither want nor expect to be anything but bassoonists. Their career opportunities consist of moving from second bassoon to first bassoon and perhaps of moving from a second-rank orchestra to a better, more prestigious one. Similarly, many medical technologists neither expect nor want to be anything but medical technologists. Their career opportunities consist of a fairly good chance of moving up to senior technician, and a very slim chance of becoming lab director. For those who make it to lab director, about 1 out of every 25 or 30 technicians, there is also the opportunity to move to a bigger, richer hospital. The district officer in India had practically no chance for professional growth except possibly to be relocated, after a three-year stint, to a bigger district.

Opportunities for specialists in an information-based business organization should be more plentiful than they are in an orchestra or hospital, let alone in the Indian civil service. But as in these organizations, they will primarily be opportunities for advancement within the specialty, and for limited advancement at that. Advancement into "management" will be the exception, for the simple reason that there will be far fewer middle-management positions to move into. This contrasts sharply with the traditional organization where, except in the research lab, the main line of advancement in rank is out of the specialty and into general management.

More than 30 years ago General Electric tackled this problem by creating "parallel opportunities" for "individual professional contributors." Many companies have followed this example. But professional specialists them-

selves have largely rejected it as a solution. To them—
and to their management colleagues—the only meaningful opportunities are promotions into management. And
the prevailing compensation structure in practically all
businesses reinforces this attitude because it is heavily
biased toward managerial positions and titles.

There are no easy answers to this problem. Some help
may come from looking at large law and consulting
firms, where even the most senior partners tend to be
specialists, and associates who will not make partner are
outplaced fairly early on. But whatever scheme is eventually developed will work only if the values and compensation structure of business are drastically changed.

The second challenge that management faces is giving its organization of specialists a common vision, a
view of the whole.

In the Indian civil service, the district officer was
expected to see the "whole" of his district. But to enable
him to concentrate on it, the government services that
arose one after the other in the nineteenth century
(forestry, irrigation, the archaeological survey, public
health and sanitation, roads) were organized outside the
administrative structure, and had virtually no contact
with the district officer. This meant that the district officer became increasingly isolated from the activities that
often had the greatest impact on—and the greatest
importance for—his district. In the end, only the provincial government or the central government in Delhi had
a view of the "whole," and it was an increasingly abstract
one at that.

A business simply cannot function this way. It needs
a view of the whole and a focus on the whole to be
shared among a great many of its professional specialists, certainly among the senior ones. And yet it will

have to accept, indeed will have to foster, the pride and professionalism of its specialists—if only because, in the absence of opportunities to move into middle management, their motivation must come from that pride and professionalism.

One way to foster professionalism, of course, is through assignments to task forces. And the information-based business will use more and more smaller self-governing units, assigning them tasks tidy enough for "a good man to get his arms around," as the old phrase has it. But to what extent should information-based businesses rotate performing specialists out of their specialties and into new ones? And to what extent will top management have to accept as its top priority making and maintaining a common vision across professional specialties?

Who will the business's managers be?

Heavy reliance on task-force teams assuages one problem. But it aggravates another: the management structure of the information-based organization. Who will the business's managers be? Will they be task-force leaders? Or will there be a two-headed monster—a specialist structure, comparable, perhaps, to the way attending physicians function in a hospital, and an administrative structure of task-force leaders?

The decisions we face on the role and function of the task-force leaders are risky and controversial. Is theirs a permanent assignment, analogous to the job of the supervisory nurse in the hospital? Or is it a function of the task that changes as the task does? Is it an assignment or a position? Does it carry any rank at all? And if it does, will the task-force leaders become in time what the product managers have been at Procter & Gamble: the basic units of management and the company's field officers? Might the task-force leaders eventually replace department heads and vice presidents?

Signs of every one of these developments exist, but there is neither a clear trend nor much understanding as to what each entails. Yet each would give rise to a different organizational structure from any we are familiar with.

Finally, the toughest problem will probably be to ensure the supply, preparation, and testing of top management people. This is, of course, an old and central dilemma as well as a major reason for the general acceptance of decentralization in large businesses in the last 40 years. But the existing business organization has a great many middle-management positions that are supposed to prepare and test a person. As a result, there are usually a good many people to choose from when filling a senior management slot. With the number of middle-management positions sharply cut, where will the information-based organization's top executives come from? What will be their preparation? How will they have been tested?

Decentralization into autonomous units will surely be even more critical than it is now. Perhaps we will even copy the German *Gruppe* in which the decentralized units are set up as separate companies with their own top managements. The Germans use this model precisely because of their tradition of promoting people in their specialties, especially in research and engineering; if they did not have available commands in near-independent subsidiaries to put people in, they would have little opportunity to train and test their most promising professionals. These subsidiaries are thus

> *With middle management sharply cut, where will the top executives come from?*

somewhat like the farm teams of a major-league baseball club.

We may also find that more and more top management jobs in big companies are filled by hiring people away from smaller companies. This is the way that major orchestras get their conductors—a young conductor earns his or her spurs in a small orchestra or opera house, only to be hired away by a larger one. And the heads of a good many large hospitals have had similar careers.

Can business follow the example of the orchestra and hospital where top management has become a separate career? Conductors and hospital administrators come out of courses in conducting or schools of hospital administration respectively. We see something of this sort in France, where large companies are often run by men who have spent their entire previous careers in government service. But in most countries this would be unacceptable to the organization (only France has the *mystique* of the *grandes écoles*). And even in France, businesses, especially large ones, are becoming too demanding to be run by people without firsthand experience and a proven success record.

Thus the entire top management process—preparation, testing, succession—will become even more problematic than it already is. There will be a growing need for experienced businesspeople to go back to school. And business schools will surely need to work out what successful professional specialists must know to prepare themselves for high-level positions as *business* executives and *business* leaders.

Since modern business enterprise first arose, after the Civil War in the United States and the Franco-Prussian War in Europe, there have been two major evolutions in the concept and structure of organizations. The first took place in the ten years between 1895 and 1905. It distinguished management from ownership and established management as work and task in its own right. This happened first in Germany, when Georg Siemens, the founder and head of Germany's premier bank, *Deutsche Bank*, saved the electrical apparatus company his cousin Werner had founded after Werner's sons and heirs had mismanaged it into near collapse. By threatening to cut off the bank's loans, he forced his cousins to turn the company's management over to professionals. A little later, J.P. Morgan, Andrew Carnegie, and John D. Rockefeller, Sr. followed suit in their massive restructurings of U.S. railroads and industries.

The second evolutionary change took place 20 years later. The development of what we still see as the modern corporation began with Pierre S. du Pont's restructuring of his family company in the early twenties and continued with Alfred P. Sloan's redesign of General Motors a few years later. This introduced the command-and-control organization of today, with its emphasis on decentralization, central service staffs,

We can identify requirements and point to problems; the job of building is still ahead.

personnel management, the whole apparatus of budgets and controls, and the important distinction between policy and operations. This stage culminated in the massive reorganization of General Electric in the early 1950s, an action that perfected the model most big businesses around the world (including Japanese organizations) still follow.[2]

Now we are entering a third period of change: the shift from the command-and-control organization, the

organization of departments and divisions, to the information-based organization, the organization of knowledge specialists. We can perceive, though perhaps only
dimly, what this organization will look like. We can
identify some of its main characteristics and requirements. We can point to central problems of values,
structure, and behavior. But the job of actually building
the information-based organization is still ahead of us—
it is the managerial challenge of the future.

Notes

1. The standard account is Philip Woodruff, *The Men Who
   Ruled India*, especially the first volume, *The Founders of
   Modern India* (New York: St. Martin's, 1954). How the system worked day by day is charmingly told in *Sowing* (New
   York: Harcourt Brace Jovanovich, 1962), volume one of
   the autobiography of Leonard Woolf (Virginia Woolf's
   husband).

2. Alfred D. Chandler, Jr. has masterfully chronicled the process in his two books *Strategy and Structure* (Cambridge:
   MIT Press, 1962) and *The Visible Hand* (Cambridge: Harvard University Press, 1977)—surely the best studies of
   the administrative history of any major institution. The
   process itself and its results were presented and analyzed
   in two of my books: *The Concept of the Corporation* (New
   York: John Day, 1946) and *The Practice of Management*
   (New York: Harper Brothers, 1954).

Originally published in January–February 1988
Reprint 88105

The Knowledge-Creating Company

IKUJIRO NONAKA

Executive Summary

IN AN ECONOMY where the only certainty is uncertainty, the one sure source of lasting competitive advantage is knowledge. And yet, few managers understand the true nature of the knowledge-creating company—let alone know how to manage it.

According to Japanese organizational theorist Ikujiro Nonaka, the problem is that most Western managers hold a too-narrow view of what knowledge is and what companies must do to exploit it. They believe that the only useful knowledge is "hard" (read: quantifiable) data. And they see the company as a kind of machine for "information processing."

But there is another way to think about knowledge and its role in business organizations. It is found most commonly at highly successful Japanese companies such as Honda, Canon, Matsushita, and Sharp. Managers at these companies recognize that creating new knowledge is not simply a matter of mechanistically "processing" objective information. Rather, it depends on tapping the tacit and often highly subjective insights, intuitions, and ideals of employees. The means for making use of such knowledge are often "soft"—taking the form of slogans, metaphors, and symbols—but they are indispensable tools for continuous innovation.

The reasons Japanese companies seem especially good at this holistic kind of knowledge creation are complicated. But the key lesson for managers is quite simple: much as manufacturers around the world have learned from Japanese manufacturing techniques, any company that wants to compete on knowledge must also learn from Japanese techniques of knowledge creation. Using vivid examples from leading Japanese companies, Nonaka proposes a fresh way to think about managerial roles and responsibilities, organizational design, and business practices in the knowledge-creating company.

I n   a n   e c o n o m y   where the only certainty is uncertainty, the one sure source of lasting competitive advantage is knowledge. When markets shift, technologies proliferate, competitors multiply, and products become obsolete almost overnight, successful companies are those that consistently create new knowledge, disseminate it widely throughout the organization, and quickly embody it in new technologies and products. These activities define the "knowledge-creating" company, whose sole business is continuous innovation.

And yet, despite all the talk about "brainpower" and "intellectual capital," few managers grasp the true nature of the knowledge-creating company—let alone know how to manage it. The reason: they misunderstand what knowledge is and what companies must do to exploit it.

Deeply ingrained in the traditions of Western management, from Frederick Taylor to Herbert Simon, is a view of the organization as a machine for "information processing." According to this view, the only useful knowledge is formal and systematic—hard (read: quantifiable) data, codified procedures, universal principles. And the key metrics for measuring the value of new knowledge are similarly hard and quantifiable— increased efficiency, lower costs, improved return on investment.

But there is another way to think about knowledge and its role in business organizations. It is found most commonly at highly successful Japanese competitors like Honda, Canon, Matsushita, NEC, Sharp, and Kao. These companies have become famous for their ability to respond quickly to customers, create new markets, rapidly develop new products, and dominate emergent technologies. The secret of their success is their unique approach to managing the creation of new knowledge.

To Western managers, the Japanese approach often seems odd or even incomprehensible. Consider the following examples:

- How is the slogan "Theory of Automobile Evolution" a meaningful design concept for a new car? And yet, this phrase led to the creation of the Honda City, Honda's innovative urban car.

- Why is a beer can a useful analogy for a personal copier? Just such an analogy caused a fundamental breakthrough in the design of Canon's revolutionary mini-copier, a product that created the personal copier market and has led Canon's successful migration from its stagnating camera business to the more lucrative field of office automation.

- What possible concrete sense of direction can a made-up word such as "optoelectronics" provide a company's product-development engineers? Under this rubric, however, Sharp has developed a reputation for creating "first products" that define new technologies and markets, making Sharp a major player in businesses ranging from color televisions to liquid crystal displays to customized integrated circuits.

In each of these cases, cryptic slogans that to a Western manager sound just plain silly—appropriate for an advertising campaign perhaps but certainly not for running a company—are in fact highly effective tools for creating new knowledge. Managers everywhere recognize the serendipitous quality of innovation. Executives at these Japanese companies are *managing* that serendipity to the benefit of the company, its employees, and its customers.

The centerpiece of the Japanese approach is the recognition that creating new knowledge is not simply a matter of "processing" objective information. Rather, it depends on tapping the tacit and often highly subjective insights, intuitions, and hunches of individual employees and making those insights available for testing and use by the company as a whole. The key to this process is personal commitment, the employees' sense of identity with the enterprise and its mission. Mobilizing that commitment and embodying tacit knowledge in actual technologies and products require managers who are as comfortable with images and symbols—slogans such as Theory of Automobile Evolution, analogies like that between a personal copier and a beer can, metaphors such as "optoelectronics"—as they are with hard numbers measuring market share, productivity, or ROI.

The more holistic approach to knowledge at many Japanese companies is also founded on another fundamental insight. A company is not a machine but a living organism. Much like an individual, it can have a collective sense of identity and fundamental purpose. This is the organizational equivalent of self-knowledge—a shared understanding of what the company stands for, where it is going, what kind of world it wants to live in, and, most important, how to make that world a reality.

In this respect, the knowledge-creating company is as much about ideals as it is about ideas. And that fact fuels innovation. The essence of innovation is to re-create the world according to a particular vision or ideal. To create new knowledge means quite literally to re-create the company and everyone in it in a nonstop process of personal and organizational self-renewal. In the knowledge-creating company, inventing new knowledge is not a specialized activity—the province of the R&D department or marketing or strategic planning. It is a way of behaving, indeed a way of being, in which everyone is a knowledge worker—that is to say, an entrepreneur.

The reasons why Japanese companies seem especially good at this kind of continuous innovation and self-renewal are complicated. But the key lesson for managers is quite simple: much as manufacturers around the world have learned from Japanese manufacturing techniques, any company that wants to compete on knowledge must also learn from Japanese techniques of knowledge creation. The experiences of the Japanese companies discussed below suggest a fresh way to think about managerial roles and responsibilities, organizational design, and business practices in the knowledge-creating company. It is an approach that puts knowledge creation exactly where it belongs: at the very center of a company's human resources strategy.

The Spiral of Knowledge

New knowledge always begins with the individual. A brilliant researcher has an insight that leads to a new patent. A middle manager's intuitive sense of market trends becomes the catalyst for an important new product concept. A shop-floor worker draws on years of experience to come up with a new process innovation. In each case, an individual's personal knowledge is transformed into organizational knowledge valuable to the company as a whole.

Making personal knowledge available to others is the central activity of the knowledge-creating company. It takes place continuously and at all levels of the organization. And as the following example suggests, sometimes it can take unexpected forms.

In 1985, product developers at the Osaka-based Matsushita Electric Company were hard at work on a new home bread-making machine. But they were having trouble getting the machine to knead dough correctly. Despite their efforts, the crust of the bread was overcooked while the inside was hardly done at all. Employees exhaustively analyzed the problem. They even compared X rays of

Creating new knowledge is as much about ideals as it is about ideas.

dough kneaded by the machine and dough kneaded by professional bakers. But they were unable to obtain any meaningful data.

Finally, software developer Ikuko Tanaka proposed a creative solution. The Osaka International Hotel had a reputation for making the best bread in Osaka. Why not use it as a model? Tanaka trained with the hotel's head baker to study his kneading technique. She observed that the baker had a distinctive way of stretching the dough. After a year of trial and error, working closely with the project's engineers, Tanaka came up with product specifications—including the addition of special ribs inside the machine—that successfully reproduced the baker's stretching technique and the quality of the bread she had learned to make at the hotel. The result: Matsushita's unique "twist dough" method and a product that in its first year set a record for sales of a new kitchen appliance.

Ikuko Tanaka's innovation illustrates a movement between two very different types of knowledge. The end point of that movement is "explicit" knowledge: the product specifications for the bread-making machine. Explicit knowledge is formal and systematic. For this reason, it can be easily communicated and shared, in product specifications or a scientific formula or a computer program.

But the starting point of Tanaka's innovation is another kind of knowledge that is not so easily expressible: "tacit" knowledge like that possessed by the chief baker at the Osaka International Hotel. Tacit knowledge is highly personal. It is hard to formalize and, therefore, difficult to communicate to others. Or in the words of the philosopher Michael Polanyi, "We can know more than we can tell." Tacit knowledge is also deeply rooted in action and in an individual's commitment to a specific context—a craft or profession, a particular technology or product market, or the activities of a work group or team.

Tacit knowledge consists partly of technical skills—the kind of informal, hard-to-pin-down skills captured in the term "know-how." A master craftsman after years of experience develops a wealth of expertise "at his fingertips." But he is often unable to articulate the scientific or technical principles behind what he knows.

At the same time, tacit knowledge has an important cognitive dimension. It consists of mental models, beliefs, and perspectives so ingrained that we take them for granted, and therefore cannot easily articulate them. For this very reason, these implicit models profoundly shape how we perceive the world around us.

The distinction between tacit and explicit knowledge suggests four basic patterns for creating knowledge in any organization:

1. From Tacit to Tacit. Sometimes, one individual shares tacit knowledge directly with another. For example, when Ikuko Tanaka apprentices herself to the head baker at the Osaka International Hotel, she learns his tacit skills through observation, imitation, and practice. They become part of her own tacit knowledge base. Put another way, she is "socialized" into the craft.

But on its own, socialization is a rather limited form of knowledge creation. True, the apprentice learns the master's skills. But neither the apprentice nor the master gain any systematic insight into their craft knowledge. Because their knowledge never becomes explicit, it cannot easily be leveraged by the organization as a whole.

2. From Explicit to Explicit. An individual can also combine discrete pieces of explicit knowledge into a new whole. For example, when a comptroller of a company collects information from throughout the organization and puts it together in a financial report, that report is new knowledge in the sense that it synthesizes information from many different sources. But this combination does not really extend the company's existing knowledge base either.

But when tacit and explicit knowledge interact, as in the Matsushita example, something powerful happens. It is precisely this exchange *between* tacit and explicit knowledge that Japanese companies are especially good at developing.

3. From Tacit to Explicit. When Ikuko Tanaka is able to articulate the foundations of her tacit knowledge of bread making, she converts it into explicit knowledge, thus allowing it to be shared with her project-development team. Another example might be the comptroller who, instead of merely compiling a conventional financial plan for his company, develops an innovative new approach to budgetary control based on his own tacit knowledge developed over years in the job.

4. From Explicit to Tacit. What's more, as new explicit knowledge is shared throughout an organization, other employees begin to internalize it—that is, they use it to broaden, extend, and reframe their own tacit knowledge. The comptroller's proposal causes a revision of the company's financial control system. Other employees use the innovation and eventually come to take it for granted as part of the background of tools and resources necessary to do their jobs.

In the knowledge-creating company, all four of these patterns exist in dynamic interaction, a kind of spiral of knowledge. Think back to Matsushita's Ikuko Tanaka:

1. First, she learns the tacit secrets of the Osaka International Hotel baker (socialization).

2. Next, she translates these secrets into explicit knowledge that she can communicate to her team members and others at Matsushita (articulation).

3. The team then standardizes this knowledge, putting it together into a manual or workbook and embodying it in a product (combination).

4. Finally, through the experience of creating a new product, Tanaka and her team members enrich their own tacit knowledge base (internalization). In particular, they come to understand in an extremely intuitive way that products like the home bread-making machine can provide genuine quality. That is, the machine must make bread that is as good as that of a professional baker.

This starts the spiral of knowledge all over again, but this time at a higher level. The new tacit insight about genuine quality developed in designing the home bread-making machine is informally conveyed to other Matsushita employees. They use it to formulate equivalent quality standards for other new Matsushita products— whether kitchen appliances, audiovisual equipment, or white goods. In this way, the organization's knowledge base grows ever broader.

Articulation (converting tacit knowledge into explicit knowledge) and internalization (using that explicit knowledge to extend one's own tacit knowledge base) are the critical steps in this spiral of knowledge. The reason is that both require the active involvement of the self—that is, personal commitment. Ikuko Tanaka's decision to apprentice herself to a master baker is one example of this commitment. Similarly, when the comptroller articulates his tacit knowledge and embodies it in a new innovation, his personal identity is directly involved in a way it is not when he merely "crunches" the numbers of a conventional financial plan.

Indeed, because tacit knowledge includes mental models and beliefs in addition to know-how, moving from the tacit to the explicit is really a process of articulating one's vision of the world—what it is and what it ought to be. When employees invent new knowledge, they are also reinventing themselves, the company, and even the world.

When managers grasp this, they realize that the appropriate tools for managing the knowledge-creating company look very different from those found at most Western companies.

From Metaphor to Model

To convert tacit knowledge into explicit knowledge means finding a way to express the inexpressible. Unfortunately, one of the most powerful management tools for doing so is also among the most frequently overlooked: the store of figurative language and symbolism that managers can draw from to articulate their intuitions and insights. At Japanese companies, this evocative and sometimes extremely poetic language figures especially prominently in product development.

In 1978, top management at Honda inaugurated the development of a new-concept car with the slogan, "Let's gamble." The phrase expressed senior executives' conviction that Honda's Civic and the Accord models were becoming too familiar. Managers also realized that along with a new postwar generation entering the car market, a new generation of young product designers was coming of age with unconventional ideas about what made a good car.

The business decision that followed from the "Let's gamble" slogan was to form a new-product development team of young engineers and designers (the average age was 27). Top management charged the team with two—and only two—instructions: first, to come up with a product concept fundamentally different from anything the company had ever done before; and second, to make a car that was inexpensive but not cheap.

This mission might sound vague, but in fact it provided the team an extremely clear sense of direction. For instance, in the early days of the project, some team members proposed designing a smaller and cheaper version of the Honda Civic—a safe and technologically feasible option. But the team quickly decided this approach contradicted the entire rationale of its mission. The only alternative was to invent something totally new.

Project team leader Hiroo Watanabe coined another slogan to express his sense of the team's ambitious challenge: Theory of Automobile Evolution. The phrase described an ideal. In effect, it posed the question: If the automobile were an organism, how should it evolve? As team members argued and discussed what Watanabe's slogan might possibly mean, they came up with an answer in the form of yet another slogan: "man-maximum, machine-minimum." This captured the team's belief that the ideal car should somehow transcend the traditional human-machine relationship. But that required challenging what Watanabe called "the reasoning of Detroit," which had sacrificed comfort for appearance.

The "evolutionary" trend the team articulated eventually came to be embodied in the image of a sphere—a car simultaneously "short" (in length) and "tall" (in height). Such a car, they reasoned, would be lighter and cheaper, but also more comfortable and more solid than traditional cars. A sphere provided the most room for the passenger while taking up the least amount of space on the road. What's more, the shape minimized the space taken up by the engine and other mechanical systems. This gave birth to a product concept the team called "Tall Boy," which eventually led to the Honda City, the company's distinctive urban car.

The Tall Boy concept totally contradicted the conventional wisdom about automobile design at the time, which emphasized long, low sedans. But the City's revolutionary styling and engineering were prophetic. The car inaugurated a whole new approach to design in the Japanese auto industry based on the man-maximum, machine-minimum concept, which has led to the new generation of "tall and short" cars now quite prevalent in Japan.

The story of the Honda City suggests how Japanese companies use figurative language at all levels of the company and in all phases of the product development process. It also begins to suggest the different kinds of figurative language and the distinctive role each plays.

One kind of figurative language that is especially important is metaphor. By "metaphor," I don't just mean a grammatical structure or allegorical expression. Rather, metaphor is a distinctive method of perception. It is a way for individuals grounded in different contexts and with different experiences to understand something intuitively through the use of imagination and symbols without the need for analysis or generalization. Through metaphors, people put together what they know in new ways and begin to express what they know but cannot yet say. As such, metaphor is highly effective in fostering direct commitment to the creative process in the early stages of knowledge creation.

Metaphor accomplishes this by merging two different and distant areas of experience into a single, inclusive image or symbol—what linguistic philosopher Max Black has aptly described as "two ideas in one phrase." By establishing a connection between two things that seem only distantly related, metaphors set up a discrepancy or conflict. Often, metaphoric images have multiple meanings, appear logically contradictory or even irrational. But far from being a weakness, this is in fact an enormous strength. For it is the very conflict that metaphors embody that jump-starts the creative process. As employees try to define more clearly the insight that the metaphor expresses, they work to reconcile the conflicting meanings. That is the first step in making the tacit explicit.

Consider the example of Hiroo Watanabe's slogan, Theory of Automobile Evolution. Like any good metaphor, it combines two ideas one wouldn't normally think of together—the automobile, which is a machine, and the theory of evolution, which refers to living organisms. And yet, this discrepancy is a fruitful platform for speculation about the characteristics of the ideal car.

But while metaphor triggers the knowledge-creation process, it alone is not enough to complete it. The next step is analogy. Whereas metaphor is mostly driven by intuition and links images that at first glance seem remote from each other, analogy is a more structured process of reconciling contradictions and making distinctions. Put another way, by clarifying how the two ideas in one phrase actually are alike and not alike, the contradictions incorporated into metaphors are harmonized by analogy. In this respect, analogy is an intermediate step between pure imagination and logical thinking.

Probably the best example of analogy comes from the development of Canon's revolutionary mini-copier. Canon designers knew that for the first personal copier to be successful, it had to be reliable. To ensure reliability, they proposed to make the product's photosensitive copier drum—which is the source of 90% of all maintenance problems—disposable. To be disposable, however, the drum would have to be easy and cheap to make. How to manufacture a throwaway drum?

The breakthrough came one day when task-force leader Hiroshi Tanaka ordered out for some beer. As the team discussed design problems over their drinks, Tanaka held one of the beer cans and wondered aloud, "How much does it cost to manufacture this can?" The question led the team to speculate whether the same process for making an aluminum beer can could be applied to the manufacture of an aluminum copier drum. By exploring how the drum actually is and is not like a beer can, the mini-copier development team was able to come up with the process technology that could manufacture an aluminum copier drum at the appropriate low cost.

Finally, the last step in the knowledge-creation process is to create an actual model. A model is far more immediately conceivable than a metaphor or an analogy. In the model, contradictions get resolved and concepts become transferable through consistent and systematic logic. The quality standards for the bread at the Osaka

International Hotel lead Matsushita to develop the right product specifications for its home bread-making machine. The image of a sphere leads Honda to its Tall Boy product concept.

Of course, terms like "metaphor," "analogy," and "model" are ideal types. In reality, they are often hard to distinguish from each other; the same phrase or image can embody more than one of the three functions. Still, the three terms capture the process by which organizations convert tacit knowledge into explicit knowledge: first, by linking contradictory things and ideas through metaphor; then, by resolving these contradictions through analogy; and, finally, by crystallizing the created concepts and embodying them in a model, which makes the knowledge available to the rest of the company.

From Chaos to Concept: Managing the Knowledge-Creating Company

Understanding knowledge creation as a process of making tacit knowledge explicit—a matter of metaphors, analogies, and models—has direct implications for how a company designs its organization and defines managerial roles and responsibilities within it. This is the "how" of the knowledge-creating company, the structures and practices that translate a company's vision into innovative technologies and products.

The fundamental principle of organizational design at the Japanese companies I have studied is redundancy—the conscious overlapping of company information, business activities, and managerial responsibilities. To Western managers, the term "redundancy," with its connotations of unnecessary duplication and waste, may sound unappealing. And yet, building a redundant organization is the first step in managing the knowledge-creating company.

Redundancy is important because it encourages frequent dialogue and communication. This helps create a "common cognitive ground" among employees and thus facilitates the transfer of

Managers must challenge tacit knowledge. Since ***employees to reexamine*** members of the organi- ***what they take for granted.*** zation share overlapping information, they can sense what others are struggling to articulate. Redundancy also spreads new explicit knowledge through the organization so it can be internalized by employees.

The organizational logic of redundancy helps explain why Japanese companies manage product development as an overlapping process where different functional divisions work together in a shared division of labor. At Canon, redundant product development goes one step further. The company organizes product-development teams according to "the principle of internal competition." A team is divided into competing groups that develop different approaches to the same project and then argue over the advantages and disadvantages of their proposals. This encourages the team to look at a project from a variety of perspectives. Under the guidance of a team leader, the team eventually develops a common understanding of the "best" approach.

In one sense, such internal competition is wasteful. Why have two or more groups of employees pursuing the same product-development project? But when responsibilities are shared, information proliferates, and the organization's ability to create and implement concepts is accelerated.

At Canon, for example, inventing the mini-copier's low-cost disposable drum resulted in new technologies that facilitated miniaturization, weight reduction, and automated assembly. These technologies were then quickly applied to other office automation products such as microfilm readers, laser printers, word processors, and typewriters. This was an important factor in diversifying Canon from cameras to office automation and in securing a competitive edge in the laser printer industry. By 1987—only five years after the mini-copier was introduced—a full 74% of Canon's revenues came from its business machines division.

Another way to build redundancy is through strategic rotation, especially between different areas of technology and between functions such as R&D and marketing. Rotation helps employees understand the business from a multiplicity of perspectives. This makes organizational knowledge more "fluid" and easier to put into practice. At Kao Corporation, a leading Japanese consumer-products manufacturer, researchers often "retire" from the R&D department by the age of 40 in order to transfer to other departments such as marketing, sales, or production. And all employees are expected to hold at least three different jobs in any given ten-year period.

Free access to company information also helps build redundancy. When information differentials exist, members of an organization can no longer interact on equal terms, which hinders the search for different interpretations of new knowledge. Thus Kao's top management does not allow any discrimination in access to information among employees. All company information (with the exception of personnel data) is stored in a single integrated database, open to any employee regardless of position.

As these examples suggest, no one department or group of experts has the exclusive responsibility for creating new knowledge in the knowledge-creating company. Senior managers, middle managers, and frontline employees all play a part. Indeed, the value of any one person's contribution is determined less by his or her location in the organizational hierarchy than by the importance of the information he or she provides to the entire knowledge-creating system.

But this is not to say that there is no differentiation among roles and responsibilities in the knowledge-creating company. In fact, creating new knowledge is the product of a dynamic interaction among three roles.

Frontline employees are immersed in the day-to-day details of particular technologies, products, or markets. No one is more expert in the realities of a company's business than they are. But while these employees are deluged with highly specific information, they often find it extremely difficult to turn that information into useful knowledge. For one thing, signals from the marketplace can be vague and ambiguous. For another, employees can become so caught up in their own narrow perspective, that they lose sight of the broader context.

What's more, even when employees *do* develop meaningful ideas and insights, it can still be difficult to communicate the import of that information to others. People don't just passively receive new knowledge, they actively interpret it to fit their own situation and perspective. Thus what makes sense in one context can change or even lose its meaning when communicated to people in a different context. As a result, there is a continual shift in meaning as new knowledge is diffused in an organization.

The confusion created by the inevitable discrepancies in meaning that occur in any organization might seem like a problem. In fact, it can be a rich source of new knowledge—*if* a company knows how to manage it. The key to doing so is continuously challenging employees to reexamine what they take for granted. Such reflection is always necessary in the knowledge-creating company, but it is especially essential during times of crisis or breakdown, when a company's traditional categories of knowledge no longer work. At such moments, ambiguity can prove extremely useful as a source of alternative meanings, a fresh way to think about things, a new sense of direction. In this respect, new knowledge is born in chaos.

The main job of managers in the knowledge-creating company is to orient this chaos toward purposeful knowledge creation. Managers do this by providing employees with a conceptual framework that helps them make sense of their own experience. This takes place at the senior management level at the top of the company and at the middle management level on company teams.

Senior managers give voice to a company's future by articulating metaphors, symbols, and concepts that orient the knowledge-creating activities of employees. They do this by asking the questions: What are we trying to learn? What do we need to know? Where should we be going? Who are we? If the job of front-line employees is to know "what is," then the job of senior executives is to know "what ought to be." Or in the words of Hiroshi Honma,

According to one Honda researcher, "Senior managers are romantics who go in quest of the ideal."

senior researcher at Honda: "Senior managers are romantics who go in quest of the ideal."

At some of the Japanese companies I have studied, CEOs talk about this role in terms of their responsibility for articulating the company's "conceptual umbrella": the grand concepts that in highly universal and abstract terms identify the common features linking seemingly disparate activities or businesses into a coherent whole. Sharp's dedication to optoelectronics is a good example.

In 1973, Sharp invented the first low-power electronic calculator by combining two key technologies—liquid crystal displays (LCDs) and complementary metal oxide semiconductors (CMOSs). Company technologists coined the term "optoelectronics" to describe this merging of microelectronics with optical technologies. The company's senior managers then took up the word and magnified its impact far beyond the R&D and engineering departments in the company.

Optoelectronics represents an image of the world that Sharp wants to live in. It is one of the key concepts articulating what the company ought to be. As such, it has become an overarching guide for the company's strategic development. Under this rubric, Sharp has moved beyond its original success in calculators to become a market leader in a broad range of products based on LCD and semiconductor technologies, including: the Electronic Organizer pocket notebook, LCD projection systems, as well as customized integrated circuits such as masked ROMs, ASICs, and CCDs (charge-coupled devices, which convert light into electronic signals).

Other Japanese companies have similar umbrella concepts. At NEC, top management has categorized the company's knowledge base in terms of a few key technologies and then developed the metaphor "C&C" (for "computers and communications"). At Kao, the umbrella concept is "surface active science," referring to techniques for coating the surface area of materials. This phrase has guided the company's diversification into products ranging from soap detergents to cosmetics to floppy disks—all natural derivatives of Kao's core knowledge base.

Another way top management provides employees with a sense of direction is by setting the standards for justifying the value of the knowledge that is constantly being developed by the organization's members. Deciding which efforts to support and develop is a highly strategic task.

In most companies, the ultimate test for measuring the value of new knowledge is economic—increased efficiency, lower costs, improved ROI. But in the knowledge-creating company, other more qualitative factors are equally important. Does the idea embody the company's vision? Is it an expression of top management's aspirations and strategic goals? Does it have the potential to build the company's organizational knowledge network?

The decision by Mazda to pursue the development of the rotary engine is a classic example of this more qualitative kind of justification. In 1974, the product-development team working on the engine was facing heavy pressure within the company to abandon the project. The rotary engine was a "gas guzzler," critics complained. It would never succeed in the marketplace.

Kenichi Yamamoto, head of the development team (and currently Mazda's chairman), argued that to stop the project would mean giving up on the company's dream of revolutionizing the combustion engine. "Let's think this way," Yamamoto proposed. "We are making history, and it is our fate to deal with this challenge." The decision to continue led to Mazda's successful rotary-engine sports car, the Savanna RX-7.

Seen from the perspective of traditional management, Yamamoto's argument about the company's "fate" sounds crazy. But in the context of the knowledge-creating company, it makes perfect sense. Yamamoto appealed to the fundamental aspirations of the company—what he termed "dedication to uncompromised value"—and to the strategy of technological leadership that senior executives had articulated. He showed how the rotary-engine project enacted the organization's commitment to its vision. Similarly, continuing the project reinforced the individual commitment of team members to that vision and to the organization.

Mazda management justified the decision to develop the rotary engine as an expression of the company's "fate."

Umbrella concepts and qualitative criteria for justification are crucial to giving a company's knowledge-creating activities a sense of direction. And yet, it is important to emphasize that a company's vision needs also to be open-ended, susceptible to a variety of different and even conflicting interpretations. At first glance, this may seem contradictory. After all, shouldn't a company's vision be unambiguous, coherent, and clear? If a vision is too unambiguous, however, it becomes more akin to an order or an instruction. And orders do not foster the high degree of personal commitment on which effective knowledge creation depends.

A more equivocal vision gives employees and work groups the freedom and autonomy to set their own goals. This is important because while the ideals of senior management are important, on their own they are not enough. The best that top management can do is to clear away any obstacles and prepare the ground for self-organizing groups or teams. Then, it is up to the teams to figure out what the ideals of the top mean in reality. Thus at Honda, a slogan as vague as "Let's gamble" and an extremely broad mission gave the Honda City product-development team a strong sense of its own identity, which led to a revolutionary new product.

Teams play a central role in the knowledge-creating company because they provide a shared context where individuals can interact with each other and engage in the constant dialogue on which effective reflection depends. Team members create new points of view through dialogue and discussion. They pool their information and examine it from various angles. Eventually, they integrate their diverse individual perspectives into a new collective perspective.

This dialogue can—indeed, should—involve considerable conflict and disagreement. It is precisely such conflict that pushes employees to question existing premises and make sense of their experience in a new way. "When people's rhythms are out of sync, quarrels occur and it's hard to bring people together," acknowledges a deputy manager for advanced technology development at Canon. "Yet if a group's rhythms are completely in unison from the beginning, it's also difficult to achieve good results."

As team leaders, middle managers are at the intersection of the vertical and horizontal flows of information in the company. They serve as a bridge between the visionary ideals of the top and the often chaotic market reality of those on the front line of the business. By creating middle-level business and product concepts, middle managers mediate between "what is" and "what should be." They remake reality according to the company's vision.

Thus at Honda, top management's decision to try something completely new took concrete form at the level of Hiroo Watanabe's product-development team in the Tall Boy product concept. At Canon, the company aspiration, "Making an excellent company through transcending the camera business," became a reality when Hiroshi Tanaka's task force developed the "Easy Maintenance" product concept, which eventually gave birth to the personal copier. And at Matsushita, the company's grand concept, "Human Electronics," came to life through the efforts of Ikuko Tanaka and others who developed the middle-range concept, "Easy Rich," and embodied it in the automatic bread-making machine.

In each of these cases, middle managers synthesized the tacit knowledge of both frontline employees and senior executives, made it explicit, and incorporated it into new technologies and products. In this respect, they are the true "knowledge engineers" of the knowledge-creating company.

Originally published in November–December 1991
Reprint 91608

Building a Learning Organization

DAVID A. GARVIN

Executive Summary

CONTINUOUS IMPROVEMENT PROGRAMS are proliferating as corporations seek to better themselves and gain an edge. Unfortunately, however, failed programs far outnumber successes, and improvement rates remain low. That's because most companies have failed to grasp a basic truth. Before people and companies can improve, they first must learn. And to do this, they need to look beyond rhetoric and high philosophy and focus on the fundamentals.

Three critical issues must be addressed before a company can truly become a learning organization, writes Harvard Business School professor David Garvin. First is the question of *meaning:* a well-grounded, easy-to-apply definition of a learning organization. Second comes *management:* clearer operational guidelines for practice. Finally, better tools for *measurement* can assess an organization's rate and level of learning.

Using these "three Ms" as a framework, Garvin defines learning organizations as skilled at five main activities: systematic problem solving, experimentation with new approaches, learning from past experience, learning from the best practices of others, and transferring knowledge quickly and efficiently throughout the organization. And since you can't manage something if you can't measure it, a complete learning audit is a must. That includes measuring cognitive and behavioral changes as well as tangible improvements in results.

No learning organization is built overnight. Success comes from carefully cultivated attitudes, commitments, and management processes that accrue slowly and steadily. The first step is to foster an environment conducive to learning. Analog Devices, Chaparral Steel, Xerox, GE, and other companies provide enlightened examples.

Continuous improvement programs are sprouting up all over as organizations strive to better themselves and gain an edge. The topic list is long and varied, and sometimes it seems as though a program a month is needed just to keep up. Unfortunately, failed programs far outnumber successes, and improvement rates remain distressingly low. Why? Because most companies have failed to grasp a basic truth. Continuous improvement requires a commitment to learning.

How, after all, can an organization improve without first learning something new? Solving a problem, introducing a product, and reengineering a process all require seeing the world in a new light and acting accordingly. In the absence of learning, companies—and individuals —simply repeat old practices. Change remains cosmetic, and improvements are either fortuitous or short-lived.

A few farsighted executives—Ray Stata of Analog Devices, Gordon Forward of Chaparral Steel, Paul Allaire of Xerox—have recognized the link between learning and continuous improvement and have begun to refocus their companies around it. Scholars too have jumped on the bandwagon, beating the drum for "learning organizations" and "knowledge-creating companies." In rapidly changing businesses like semiconductors and consumer electronics, these ideas are fast taking hold. Yet despite the encouraging signs, the topic in large part remains murky, confused, and difficult to penetrate.

Meaning, Management, and Measurement

Scholars are partly to blame. Their discussions of learning organizations have often been reverential and utopian, filled with near mystical terminology. Paradise, they would have you believe, is just around the corner. Peter Senge, who popularized learning organizations in his book *The Fifth Discipline*, described them as places "where people continually expand their capacity to create the results they truly desire, where new and expansive patterns of thinking are nurtured, where collective aspiration is set free, and where people are continually learning how to learn together."[1] To achieve these ends, Senge suggested the use of five "component technologies": systems thinking, personal mastery, mental models, shared vision, and team learning. In a similar spirit, Ikujiro Nonaka characterized knowledge-creating companies as places where "inventing new knowledge is not a specialized activity . . . it is a way of behaving, indeed, a way of being, in which everyone is a knowledge worker."[2] Nonaka suggested that companies use metaphors and organizational redundancy to focus thinking, encourage dialogue, and make tacit, instinctively understood ideas explicit.

Sound idyllic? Absolutely. Desirable? Without question. But does it provide a framework for action? Hardly. The recommendations are far too abstract, and too many questions remain unanswered. How, for example, will managers know when their companies have become learning organizations? What concrete changes in behavior are required? What policies and programs must be in place? How do you get from here to there?

Most discussions of learning organizations finesse these issues. Their focus is high philosophy and grand themes, sweeping metaphors rather than the gritty details of practice. Three critical issues are left unresolved; yet each is essential for effective implementation. First is the question of *meaning*. We need a plausible, well-grounded definition of learning organizations; it must be actionable and easy to apply. Second is the question of *management*. We need clearer guidelines for practice, filled with operational advice rather than high aspirations. And third is the question of *measurement*. We need better tools for assessing an organization's rate and level of learning to ensure that gains have in fact been made.

Once these "three Ms" are addressed, managers will have a firmer foundation for launching learning organizations. Without this groundwork, progress is unlikely, and for the simplest of reasons. For learning to become a meaningful corporate goal, it must first be understood.

What Is a Learning Organization?

Surprisingly, a clear definition of learning has proved to be elusive over the years. Organizational theorists have studied learning for a long time; the accompanying quotations suggest that there is still considerable disagreement (see "Definitions of Organizational Learning" on page 77). Most scholars view organizational learning as a process that unfolds over time and link it with knowledge acquisition and improved performance. But they differ on other important matters.

Some, for example, believe that behavioral change is required for learning; others insist that new ways of thinking are enough. Some cite information processing as the mechanism through which learning takes place; others propose shared insights, organizational routines, even memory. And some think that organizational learning is common, while others believe that flawed, self-serving interpretations are the norm.

How can we discern among this cacophony of voices yet build on earlier insights? As a first step, consider the following definition:

A learning organization is an organization skilled at creating, acquiring, and transferring knowledge, and at modifying its behavior to reflect new knowledge and insights.

This definition begins with a simple truth: new ideas are essential if learning is to take place. Sometimes they are created de novo, through flashes of insight or creativity; at other times they arrive from outside the organization or are communicated by knowledgeable insiders. Whatever their source, these ideas are the trigger for organizational improvement. But they cannot by themselves create a learning organization. *Without accompanying changes in the way that work gets done, only the potential for improvement exists.*

This is a surprisingly stringent test for it rules out a number of obvious candidates for learning organizations. Many universities fail to qualify, as do many consulting firms. Even General Motors, despite its recent efforts to improve performance, is found wanting. All of these organizations have been effective at creating or acquiring new knowledge but notably less successful in applying that knowledge to their own activities. Total quality management, for example, is now taught at many business schools, yet the number using it to guide their own decision making is very small. Organizational consultants advise clients on social dynamics and small-group behavior but are notorious for their own infighting and factionalism. And GM, with a few exceptions (like Saturn and NUMMI), has had little success in revamping its manufacturing practices, even though its managers are experts on lean manufacturing, JIT production, and the requirements for improved quality of work life.

Organizations that do pass the definitional test—Honda, Corning, and General Electric come quickly to mind—have, by contrast, become adept at translating new knowledge into new ways of behaving. These companies actively manage the learning process to ensure that it occurs by design rather than by chance. Distinctive policies and practices are responsible for their success; they form the building blocks of learning organizations.

Building Blocks

Learning organizations are skilled at five main activities: systematic problem solving, experimentation with new approaches, learning from their own experience and past history, learning from the experiences and best practices of others, and transferring knowledge quickly and efficiently throughout the organization. Each is accompanied by a distinctive mind-set, tool kit, and pattern of behavior. Many companies practice these activities to some degree. But few are consistently successful because they rely largely on happenstance and isolated examples. By creating systems and processes that support these activities and integrate them into the fabric of daily operations, companies can manage their learning more effectively.

1. Systematic problem solving. This first activity rests heavily on the philosophy and methods of the quality movement. Its underlying ideas, now widely accepted, include:

- Relying on the scientific method, rather than guesswork, for diagnosing problems (what Deming calls the "Plan, Do, Check, Act" cycle, and others refer to as "hypothesis-generating, hypothesis-testing" techniques).

- Insisting on data, rather than assumptions, as background for decision making (what quality practitioners call "fact-based management").

- Using simple statistical tools (histograms, Pareto charts, correlations, cause-and-effect diagrams) to organize data and draw inferences.

Most training programs focus primarily on problem-solving techniques, using exercises and practical examples. These tools are relatively straightforward and easily communicated; the necessary mind-set, however, is more difficult to establish. Accuracy and precision are essential for learning. Employees must therefore become more disciplined in their thinking and more attentive to details. They must continually ask, "How do we know that's true?", recognizing that close enough is not good enough if real learning is to take place. They must push beyond obvious symptoms to assess underlying causes, often collecting evidence when conventional wisdom says it is unnecessary. Otherwise, the organization will remain a prisoner of "gut facts" and sloppy reasoning, and learning will be stifled.

Xerox has mastered this approach on a companywide scale. In 1983, senior managers launched the company's Leadership Through Quality initiative; since then, all employees have been trained in small-group activities and problem-solving techniques. Today a six-step process is used for virtually all decisions (see "Xerox's Problem-Solving Process"). Employees are provided with tools in four areas: generating ideas and collecting information (brainstorming, interviewing, surveying); reaching consensus (list reduction, rating forms, weighted voting); analyzing and displaying data (cause-and-effect diagrams, force-field analysis); and planning actions (flow charts, Gantt charts). They then practice these tools during training sessions that last several days. Training is presented in "family groups," members of the same department or business-unit team, and the tools are applied to real problems facing the group. The result of this process has been a common vocabulary and a consistent, companywide approach to problem solving. Once employees have been trained, they are expected to use the techniques at all meetings, and no topic is off-limits. When a high-level group was formed to review Xerox's organizational structure and suggest alternatives, it employed the very same process and tools.[3]

2. Experimentation. This activity involves the systematic searching for and testing of new knowledge. Using the scientific method is essential, and there are

Xerox's Problem-Solving Process

Step	Questions to Be Answered	Expansion/ Divergence	Contraction/ Convergence	What's Next to Go to the Next Step
1. Identify and select problem	What do we want to change?	Lots of problems for consideration	One problem statement, one "desired state" agreed upon	Identification of the gap "Desired state" described in observable terms
2. Analyze problem	What's preventing us from reaching the "desired state"?	Lots of potential causes identified	Key cause(s) identified and verified	Key cause(s) documented and ranked
3. Generate potential solutions	How *could* we make the change?	Lots of ideas on how to solve the problem	Potential solutions clarified	Solution list
4. Select and plan the solution	What's the *best* way to do it?	Lots of criteria for evaluating potential solutions Lots of ideas on how to implement and evaluate the selected solution	Criteria to use for evaluating solution agreed upon Implementation and evaluation plans agreed upon	Plan for making and monitoring the change Measurement criteria to evaluate solution effectiveness
5. Implement the solution	Are we following the plan?		Implementation of agreed-on contingency plans (if necessary)	Solution in place
6. Evaluate the solution	How well did it work?		Effectiveness of solution agreed upon Continuing problems (if any) identified	Verification that the problem is solved, or Agreement to address continuing problems

obvious parallels to systematic problem solving. But unlike problem solving, experimentation is usually motivated by opportunity and expanding horizons, not by current difficulties. It takes two main forms: ongoing programs and one-of-a-kind demonstration projects.

Ongoing programs normally involve a continuing series of small experiments, designed to produce incremental gains in knowledge. They are the mainstay of most continuous improvement programs and are especially common on the shop floor. Corning, for example, experiments continually with diverse raw materials and new formulations to increase yields and provide better grades of glass. Allegheny Ludlum, a specialty steelmaker, regularly examines new rolling methods and improved technologies to raise productivity and reduce costs.

Successful ongoing programs share several characteristics. First, they work hard to ensure a steady flow of new ideas, even if they must be imported from outside the organization. Chaparral Steel sends its first-line supervisors on sabbaticals around the globe, where they visit academic and industry leaders, develop an understanding of new work practices and technologies, then bring what they've learned back to the company and apply it to daily operations. In large part as a result of these initiatives, Chaparral is one of the five lowest cost steel plants in the world. GE's Impact Program originally sent manufacturing managers to Japan to study factory innovations, such as quality circles and kanban cards, and then apply them in their own organizations; today Europe is the destination,

> *Allegheny Ludlum regularly examines new rolling methods and improved technologies.*

and productivity improvement practices the target. The program is one reason GE has recorded productivity gains averaging nearly 5% over the last four years.

Successful ongoing programs also require an incentive system that favors risk taking. Employees must feel that the benefits of experimentation exceed the costs; otherwise, they will not participate. This creates a difficult challenge for managers, who are trapped between two perilous extremes. They must maintain accountability and control over experiments without stifling creativity by unduly penalizing employees for failures. Allegheny Ludlum has perfected this juggling act: it keeps expensive, high-impact experiments off the scorecard used to evaluate managers but requires prior approvals from four senior vice presidents. The result has been a history of productivity improvements annually averaging 7% to 8%.

Finally, ongoing programs need managers and employees who are trained in the skills required to perform and evaluate experiments. These skills are seldom intuitive and must usually be learned. They cover a broad sweep: statistical methods, like design of experiments, that efficiently compare a large number of alternatives; graphical techniques, like process analysis, that are essential for redesigning work flows; and creativity techniques, like storyboarding and role playing, that keep novel ideas flowing. The most effective training programs are tightly focused and feature a small set of techniques tailored to employees' needs. Training in design of experiments, for example, is useful for manufacturing engineers, while creativity techniques are well suited to development groups.

Demonstration projects are usually larger and more complex than ongoing experiments. They involve holistic, systemwide changes, introduced at a single site, and are often undertaken with the goal of developing new organizational capabilities. Because these projects represent a sharp break from the past, they are usually designed from scratch, using a "clean slate" approach. General Foods's Topeka plant, one of the first high-commitment work systems in this country, was a pioneering demonstration project initiated to introduce the idea of self-managing teams and high levels of worker autonomy; a more recent example, designed to rethink small-car development, manufacturing, and sales, is GM's Saturn Division.

Demonstration projects share a number of distinctive characteristics:

- They are usually the first projects to embody principles and approaches that the organization hopes to adopt later on a larger scale. For this reason, they are more transitional efforts than endpoints and involve considerable "learning by doing." Mid-course corrections are common.

- They implicitly establish policy guidelines and decision rules for later projects. Managers must therefore be sensitive to the precedents they are setting and must send strong signals if they expect to establish new norms.

- They often encounter severe tests of commitment from employees who wish to see whether the rules have, in fact, changed.

- They are normally developed by strong multifunctional teams reporting directly to senior management. (For projects targeting employee involvement

or quality of work life, teams should be multilevel as
well.)

- They tend to have only limited impact on the rest of
the organization if they are not accompanied by
explicit strategies for transferring learning.

All of these characteristics appeared in a demonstration project launched by Copeland Corporation, a highly
successful compressor manufacturer, in the mid-1970s.
Matt Diggs, then the new CEO, wanted to transform the
company's approach to
manufacturing. Previ-
ously, Copeland had
machined and assembled
all products in a single
facility. Costs were high, and quality was marginal. The
problem, Diggs felt, was too much complexity.

*Successful programs
require an incentive system
that favors risk taking.*

At the outset, Diggs assigned a small, multifunctional
team the task of designing a "focused factory" dedicated
to a narrow, newly developed product line. The team
reported directly to Diggs and took three years to complete its work. Initially, the project budget was $10 mil-
lion to $12 million; that figure was repeatedly revised as
the team found, through experience and with Diggs's
prodding, that it could achieve dramatic improvements.
The final investment, a total of $30 million, yielded
unanticipated breakthroughs in reliability testing, automatic tool adjustment, and programmable control. All
were achieved through learning by doing.

The team set additional precedents during the plant's
start-up and early operations. To dramatize the importance of quality, for example, the quality manager was
appointed second-in-command, a significant move
upward. The same reporting relationship was used at all

subsequent plants. In addition, Diggs urged the plant manager to ramp up slowly to full production and resist all efforts to proliferate products. These instructions were unusual at Copeland, where the marketing department normally ruled. Both directives were quickly tested; management held firm, and the implications were felt throughout the organization. Manufacturing's stature improved, and the company as a whole recognized its competitive contribution. One observer commented, "Marketing had always run the company, so they couldn't believe it. The change was visible at the highest levels, and it went down hard."

Once the first focused factory was running smoothly —it seized 25% of the market in two years and held its edge in reliability for over a decade—Copeland built four more factories in quick succession. Diggs assigned members of the initial project to each factory's design team to ensure that early learnings were not lost; these people later rotated into operating assignments. Today focused factories remain the cornerstone of Copeland's manufacturing strategy and a continuing source of its cost and quality advantages.

Whether they are demonstration projects like Copeland's or ongoing programs like Allegheny Ludlum's, all forms of experimentation seek the same end: moving from superficial knowledge to deep understanding. At its simplest, the distinction is between knowing how things are done and knowing why they occur. Knowing how is partial knowledge; it is rooted in norms of behavior, standards of practice, and settings of equipment. Knowing why is more fundamental: it captures underlying cause-and-effect relationships and accommodates exceptions, adaptations, and unforeseen events. The ability to control temperatures and pressures to align grains of silicon and form silicon steel is an example of knowing how; understanding the chemical and physical process that produces the alignment is knowing why.

Further distinctions are possible, as the insert "Stages of Knowledge" suggests. Operating knowledge can be arrayed in a hierarchy, moving from limited understanding and the ability to make few distinctions to more complete understanding in which all contingencies are anticipated and controlled. In this context, experimentation and problem solving foster learning by pushing organizations up the hierarchy, from lower to higher stages of knowledge.

3. Learning from past experience. Companies must review their successes and failures, assess them systematically, and record the lessons in a form that employees find open and accessible. One expert has called this process the "Santayana Review," citing the famous philosopher George Santayana, who coined the phrase "Those who cannot remember the past are condemned to repeat it." Unfortunately, too many managers today are indifferent, even hostile, to the past, and by failing to reflect on it, they let valuable knowledge escape.

A study of more than 150 new products concluded that "the knowledge gained from failures [is] often instrumental in achieving subsequent successes. . . . In the simplest terms, failure is the ultimate teacher."[4] IBM's 360 computer series, for example, one of the most popular and profitable ever built, was based on the technology of the failed Stretch computer that preceded it. In this case, as in many others, learning occurred by chance rather than by careful planning. A few companies, however, have established processes that require their managers to periodically think about the past and learn from their mistakes.

Boeing did so immediately after its difficulties with the 737 and 747 plane programs. Both planes were introduced with much fanfare and also with serious problems. To ensure that the problems were not repeated, senior managers commissioned a high-level employee group, called Project Homework, to compare the development processes of the 737 and 747 with those of the 707 and 727, two of the company's most profitable planes. The group was asked to develop a set of "lessons learned" that could be used on future projects. After working for three years, they produced hundreds of recommendations and an inch-thick booklet. Several members of the team were then transferred to the 757 and 767 start-ups, and guided by experience, they produced the most successful, error-free launches in Boeing's history.

Other companies have used a similar retrospective approach. Like Boeing, Xerox studied its product development process, examining three troubled products in an effort to understand why the company's new business initiatives failed so often. Arthur D. Little, the consulting company, focused on its past successes. Senior management invited ADL consultants from around the world to a two-day "jamboree," featuring booths and presentations documenting a wide range of the company's most successful practices, publications, and techniques. British Petroleum went even further and established the post-project appraisal unit to review major investment projects, write up case studies, and derive lessons for planners that were then incorporated into revisions of the company's planning guidelines. A five-person unit reported to the board of directors and reviewed six projects annually. The bulk of the time was spent in the field

interviewing managers.[5] This type of review is now conducted regularly at the project level.

At the heart of this approach, one expert has
observed, "is a mind-set that . . . enables companies to
recognize the value of productive failure as contrasted
with unproductive success. A productive failure is one
that leads to insight, understanding, and thus an addition to the commonly held wisdom of the organization.
An unproductive success occurs when something goes
well, but nobody knows how or why."[6] IBM's legendary
founder, Thomas Wat-
son, Sr., apparently
understood the distinc-
tion well. Company lore
has it that a young man-
ager, after losing $10 million in a risky venture, was
called into Watson's office. The young man, thoroughly
intimidated, began by saying, "I guess you want my res-
ignation." Watson replied, "You can't be serious. We just
spent $10 million educating you."

*Enthusiastic borrowing is
replacing the "not invented
here" syndrome.*

Fortunately, the learning process need not be so
expensive. Case studies and post-project reviews like
those of Xerox and British Petroleum can be performed
with little cost other than managers' time. Companies
can also enlist the help of faculty and students at local
colleges or universities; they bring fresh perspectives and
view internships and case studies as opportunities to
gain experience and increase their own learning. A few
companies have established computerized data banks to
speed up the learning process. At Paul Revere Life Insurance, management requires all problem-solving teams to
complete short registration forms describing their proposed projects if they hope to qualify for the company's
award program. The company then enters the forms

into its computer system and can immediately retrieve a listing of other groups of people who have worked or are working on the topic, along with a contact person. Relevant experience is then just a telephone call away.

4. Learning from others. Of course, not all learning comes from reflection and self-analysis. Sometimes the most powerful insights come from looking outside one's immediate environment to gain a new perspective. Enlightened managers know that even companies in completely different businesses can be fertile sources of ideas and catalysts for creative thinking. At these organizations, enthusiastic borrowing is replacing the "not invented here" syndrome. Milliken calls the process SIS, for "Steal Ideas Shamelessly"; the broader term for it is benchmarking.

According to one expert, "benchmarking is an ongoing investigation and learning experience that ensures that best industry practices are uncovered, analyzed, adopted, and implemented."[7] The greatest benefits come from studying practices, the way that work gets done, rather than results, and from involving line managers in the process. Almost anything can be benchmarked. Xerox, the concept's creator, has applied it to billing, warehousing, and automated manufacturing. Milliken has been even more creative: in an inspired moment, it benchmarked Xerox's approach to benchmarking.

Unfortunately, there is still considerable confusion about the requirements for successful benchmarking. Benchmarking is not "industrial tourism," a series of ad hoc visits to companies that have received favorable publicity or won quality awards. Rather, it is a disciplined process that begins with a thorough search to identify best-practice organizations, continues with careful study of one's own practices and performance, progresses through systematic site visits and interviews, and concludes with an analysis of results, development of recommendations, and implementation. While time-consuming, the process need not be terribly expensive. AT&T's Benchmarking Group estimates that a moderate-sized project takes four to six months and incurs out-of-pocket costs of $20,000 (when personnel costs are included, the figure is three to four times higher).

Benchmarking is one way of gaining an outside perspective; another, equally fertile source of ideas is customers. Conversations with customers invariably stimulate learning; they are, after all, experts in what they do. Customers can provide up-to-date product information, competitive comparisons, insights into changing preferences, and immediate feedback about service and patterns of use. And companies need these insights at all levels, from the executive suite to the shop floor. At Motorola, members of the Operating and Policy Committee, including the CEO, meet personally and on a regular basis with customers. At Worthington Steel, all machine operators make periodic, unescorted trips to customers' factories to discuss their needs.

Sometimes customers can't articulate their needs or remember even the most recent problems they have had with a product or service. If that's the case, managers must observe them in action. Xerox employs a number of anthropologists at its Palo Alto Research Center to observe users of new document products in their offices. Digital Equipment has developed an interactive process called "contextual inquiry" that is used by software engineers to observe users of new technologies as they go about their work. Milliken has created "first-delivery teams" that accompany the first shipment of all products; team members follow the product through the customer's production process to see how it is used and then develop ideas for further improvement.

Whatever the source of outside ideas, learning will only occur in a receptive environment. Managers can't be defensive and must be open to criticism or bad news. This is a difficult challenge, but it is essential for success. Companies that approach customers assuming that "we must be right, they have to be wrong" or visit other organizations certain that "they can't teach us anything" seldom learn very much. Learning organizations, by contrast, cultivate the art of open, attentive listening.

5. Transferring knowledge. For learning to be more than a local affair, knowledge must spread quickly and efficiently throughout the organization. Ideas carry maximum impact when they are shared broadly rather than held in a few hands. A variety of mechanisms spur this process, including written, oral, and visual reports, site visits and tours, personnel rotation programs, education and training programs, and standardization programs. Each has distinctive strengths and weaknesses.

Reports and tours are by far the most popular mediums. Reports serve many purposes: they summarize findings, provide checklists of dos and don'ts, and describe important processes and events. They cover a multitude of topics, from benchmarking studies to accounting conventions to newly discovered marketing techniques. Today written reports are often supplemented by videotapes, which offer greater immediacy and fidelity.

Tours are an equally popular means of transferring knowledge, especially for large, multidivisional organizations with multiple sites. The most effective tours are tailored to different audiences and needs. To introduce its managers to the distinctive manufacturing practices of New United Motor Manufacturing Inc. (NUMMI), its joint venture with Toyota, General Motors developed a series of specialized tours. Some were geared to upper and middle managers, while others were aimed at lower ranks. Each tour described the policies, practices, and systems that were most relevant to that level of management.

Despite their popularity, reports and tours are relatively cumbersome ways of transferring knowledge. The gritty details that lie behind complex management concepts are difficult to communicate secondhand. Absorbing facts by reading them or seeing them demonstrated is one thing; experiencing them personally is quite another. As a leading cognitive scientist has observed, "It is very difficult to become knowledgeable in a passive way. Actively experiencing something is considerably more valuable than having it described."[8] For this reason, personnel rotation programs are one of the most powerful methods of transferring knowledge.

Learning organizations cultivate the art of open, attentive listening. Managers must be open to criticism.

In many organizations, expertise is held locally: in a particularly skilled computer technician, perhaps, a savvy global brand manager, or a division head with a track record of successful joint ventures. Those in daily contact with these experts benefit enormously from their skills, but their field of influence is relatively narrow. Transferring them to different parts of the organization helps share the wealth. Transfers may be from division to division, department to department, or facility to facility; they may involve senior, middle, or first-level managers. A supervisor experienced in just-in-time production, for example, might move to another factory to apply the methods there, or a successful division manager might transfer to a lagging division to invigorate it with already proven ideas. The CEO of Time Life used the latter approach when he shifted the president of the company's music division, who had orchestrated several years of rapid growth and high profits through innovative marketing, to the presidency of the book division, where profits were flat because of continued reliance on traditional marketing concepts.

Line to staff transfers are another option. These are most effective when they allow experienced managers to distill what they have learned and diffuse it across the company in the form of new standards, policies, or training programs. Consider how PPG used just such a transfer to advance its human resource practices around the concept of high-commitment work systems. In 1986, PPG constructed a new float-glass plant in Chehalis, Washington; it employed a radically new technology as well as innovations in human resource management that were developed by the plant manager and his staff. All workers were organized into small, self-managing teams with responsibility for work assignments, scheduling, problem solving and improvement, and peer review. After several years running the factory, the plant manager was promoted to director of human resources for the entire glass group. Drawing on his experiences at Chehalis, he developed a training program geared toward first-level supervisors that taught

GTE proved knowledge is more likely to be transferred effectively when the right incentives are in place.

the behaviors needed to manage employees in a partici-
pative, self-managing environment.

As the PPG example suggests, education and training
programs are powerful tools for transferring knowledge.
But for maximum effectiveness, they must be linked
explicitly to implementation. All too often, trainers
assume that new knowledge will be applied without taking concrete steps to ensure that trainees actually follow
through. Seldom do trainers provide opportunities for
practice, and few programs consciously promote the
application of their teachings after employees have
returned to their jobs.

Xerox and GTE are exceptions. As noted earlier,
when Xerox introduced problem-solving techniques to
its employees in the 1980s, everyone, from the top to
the bottom of the organization, was taught in small
departmental or divisional groups led by their immediate superior. After an introduction to concepts and
techniques, each group applied what they learned to a
real-life work problem. In a similar spirit, GTE's Quality:
The Competitive Edge program was offered to teams of
business-unit presidents and the managers reporting to
them. At the beginning of the 3-day course, each team
received a request from a company officer to prepare a
complete quality plan for their unit, based on the course
concepts, within 60 days. Discussion periods of two to
three hours were set aside during the program so that
teams could begin working on their plans. After the
teams submitted their reports, the company officers
studied them, and then the teams implemented them.
This GTE program produced dramatic improvements in
quality, including a recent semifinalist spot in the
Baldrige Awards.

The GTE example suggests another important guide-

line: knowledge is more likely to be transferred effectively when the right incentives are in place. If employees know that their plans will be evaluated and implemented—in other words, that their learning will be
applied—progress is far more likely. At most companies,
the status quo is well entrenched; only if managers and
employees see new ideas as being in their own best
interest will they accept them gracefully. AT&T has
developed a creative approach that combines strong
incentives with information sharing. Called the Chairman's Quality Award (CQA), it is an internal quality
competition modeled on the Baldrige prize but with an
important twist: awards are given not only for absolute
performance (using the same 1,000-point scoring system
as Baldrige) but also for improvements in scoring from
the previous year. Gold, silver, and bronze Improvement
Awards are given to units that have improved their
scores 200, 150, and 100 points, respectively. These
awards provide the incentive for change. An accompanying Pockets of Excellence program simplifies knowledge
transfer. Every year, it identifies every unit within the
company that has scored at least 60% of the possible
points in each award category and then publicizes the
names of these units using written reports and electronic mail.

Measuring Learning

Managers have long known that "if you can't measure it,
you can't manage it." This maxim is as true of learning as
it is of any other corporate objective. Traditionally, the
solution has been "learning curves" and "manufacturing
progress functions." Both concepts date back to the discovery, during the 1920s and 1930s, that the costs of air-
frame manufacturing fell predictably with increases in

cumulative volume. These increases were viewed as proxies for greater manufacturing knowledge, and most early studies examined their impact on the costs of direct labor. Later studies expanded the focus, looking at total manufacturing costs and the impact of experience in other industries, including shipbuilding, oil refining, and consumer electronics. Typically, learning rates were in the 80% to 85% range (meaning that with a doubling of cumulative production, costs fell to 80% to 85% of their previous level), although there was wide variation.

Firms like the Boston Consulting Group raised these ideas to a higher level in the 1970s. Drawing on the logic of learning curves, they argued that industries as a whole faced "experience curves," costs and prices that fell by predictable amounts as industries grew and their total production increased. With this observation, consultants suggested, came an iron law of competition. To enjoy the benefits of experience, companies would have to rapidly increase their production ahead of competitors to lower prices and gain market share.

Both learning and experience curves are still widely used, especially in the aerospace, defense, and electronics industries. Boeing, for instance, has established learning curves for every workstation in its assembly plant; they assist in monitoring productivity, determining work flows and staffing levels, and setting prices and profit margins on new airplanes. Experience curves are common in semiconductors and consumer electronics, where they are used to forecast industry costs and prices.

For companies hoping to become learning organizations, however, these measures are incomplete. They focus on only a single measure of output (cost or price) and ignore learning that affects other competitive variables, like quality, delivery, or new product intro ductions. They suggest only one possible learning driver (total production volumes) and ignore both the possibility of learning in mature industries, where output is flat, and the possibility that learning might be driven by other sources, such as new technology or the challenge posed by competing products. Perhaps most important, they tell us little about the sources of learning or the levers of change.

Another measure has emerged in response to these concerns. Called the "half-life" curve, it was originally developed by Analog Devices, a leading semiconductor manufacturer, as a way of comparing internal improvement rates. A half-life curve measures the time it takes to achieve a 50% improvement in a specified performance measure. When represented graphically, the performance measure (defect rates, on-time delivery, time to market) is plotted on the vertical axis, using a logarithmic scale, and the time scale (days, months, years) is plotted horizontally. Steeper slopes then represent faster learning (see the exhibit "The Half-Life Curve" for an illustration).

The logic is straightforward. Companies, divisions, or departments that take less time to improve must be learning faster than their peers. In the long run, their short learning cycles will translate into superior performance. The 50% target is a measure of convenience; it was derived empirically from studies of successful improvement processes at a wide range of companies. Half-life curves are also flexible. Unlike learning and experience curves, they work on any output measure, and they are not confined to costs or prices. In addition, they are easy to operationalize, they provide a simple measuring stick, and they allow for ready comparison among groups.

Yet even half-life curves have an important weakness: they focus solely on results. Some types of knowledge take years to digest, with few visible changes in performance for long periods. Creating a total quality culture, for instance, or developing new approaches to product development are difficult systemic changes. Because of their long gestation periods, half-life curves or any other measures focused solely on results are unlikely to capture any short-run learning that has occurred. A more comprehensive framework is needed to track progress.

Organizational learning can usually be traced through three overlapping stages. The first step is cognitive. Members of the organization are exposed to new ideas, expand their knowledge, and begin to think differently. The second step is behavioral. Employees

---

The Half-Life Curve

Analog Devices has used half-life curves to compare the performance of its divisions. Here monthly data on customer service are graphed for seven divisions. Division C is the clear winner: even though it started with high proportion of late deliveries, its rapid learning rate led eventually to the best absolute performance. Divisions D, E, and G have been far less successful, with little or no improvement in on-time service over the period.

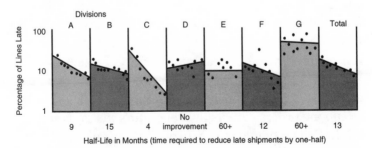

Source: Ray Stata, "Organizational Learning—The Key to Management Innovation," Sloan Management Review, Spring 1989, p. 72.

begin to internalize new insights and alter their behavior. And the third step is performance improvement, with changes in behavior leading to measurable improvements in results: superior quality, better delivery, increased market share, or other tangible gains. Because cognitive and behavioral changes typically precede improvements in performance, a complete learning audit must include all three.

Surveys, questionnaires, and interviews are useful for this purpose. At the cognitive level, they would focus on attitudes and depth of understanding. Have employees truly understood the meaning of self-direction and teamwork, or are the terms still unclear? At PPG, a team of human resource experts periodically audits every manufacturing plant, including extensive interviews with shop-floor employees, to ensure that the concepts are well understood. Have new approaches to customer service been fully accepted? At its 1989 Worldwide Marketing Managers' Meeting, Ford presented participants with a series of hypothetical situations in which customer complaints were in conflict with short-term dealer or company profit goals and asked how they would respond. Surveys like these are the first step toward identifying changed attitudes and new ways of thinking.

To assess behavioral changes, surveys and questionnaires must be supplemented by direct observation. Here the proof is in the doing, and there is no substitute for seeing employees in action. Domino's Pizza uses "mystery shoppers" to assess managers' commitment to customer service at its individual stores; L.L. Bean places telephone orders with its own operators to assess service levels. Other companies invite outside consultants to visit, attend meetings, observe employees in action, and then report what they have learned. In many ways, this approach mirrors that of examiners for the Baldrige Award, who make several-day site visits to semifinalists to see whether the companies' deeds match the words on their applications.

Finally, a comprehensive learning audit also measures performance. Half-life curves or other performance measures are essential for ensuring that cognitive and behavioral changes have actually produced results. Without them, companies would lack a rationale for investing in learning and the assurance that learning was serving the organization's ends.

First Steps

Learning organizations are not built overnight. Most successful examples are the products of carefully cultivated attitudes, commitments, and management processes that have accrued slowly and steadily over time. Still, some changes can be made immediately. Any company that wishes to become a learning organization can begin by taking a few simple steps.

The first step is to foster an environment that is conducive to learning. There must be time for reflection and analysis, to think about strategic plans, dissect customer needs, assess current work systems, and invent new products. Learning is difficult when employees are harried or rushed; it tends to be driven out by the pressures of the moment. Only if top management explicitly frees up employees' time for the purpose does learning occur with any frequency. That time will be doubly productive if employees possess the skills to use it wisely. Training in brainstorming, problem solving, evaluating experiments, and other core learning skills is therefore essential.

Another powerful lever is to open up boundaries and stimulate the exchange of ideas. Boundaries inhibit the flow of information; they keep individuals and groups isolated and reinforce preconceptions. Opening up boundaries, with conferences, meetings, and project teams, which either cross organizational levels or link the company and its customers and suppliers, ensures a fresh flow of ideas and the chance to consider competing perspectives. General Electric CEO Jack Welch considers this to be such a powerful stimulant of change that he has made "boundarylessness" a cornerstone of the company's strategy for the 1990s.

Once managers have established a more supportive, open environment, they can create learning forums. These are programs or events designed with explicit learning goals in mind, and they can take a variety of forms: strategic reviews, which examine the changing competitive environment and the company's product portfolio, technology, and market positioning; systems audits, which review the health of large, cross-functional processes and delivery systems; internal benchmarking reports, which identify and compare best-in-class activities within the organization; study missions, which are dispatched to leading organizations around the world to better understand their performance and distinctive skills; and jamborees or symposiums, which bring together customers, suppliers, outside experts, or internal groups to share ideas and learn from one another. Each of these activities fosters learning by requiring employees to wrestle with new knowledge and consider its implications. Each can also be tailored to business needs. A consumer goods company, for example, might sponsor a study mission to Europe to learn more about distribution methods within the newly unified Common Market, while a high-technology company might launch a systems audit to review its new product development process.

Together these efforts help to eliminate barriers that impede learning and begin to move learning higher on the organizational agenda. They also suggest a subtle shift in focus, away from continuous improvement and toward a commitment to learning. Coupled with a better understanding of the "three Ms," the meaning, management, and measurement of learning, this shift provides a solid foundation for building learning organizations.

Definitions of Organizational Learning

SCHOLARS HAVE PROPOSED a variety of definitions of organizational learning. Here is a small sample:

Organizational learning means the process of improving actions through better knowledge and understanding.
C. Marlene Fiol and Marjorie A. Lyles, "Organizational Learning," *Academy of Management Review*, October 1985.

An entity learns if, through its processing of information, the range of its potential behaviors is changed.
George P. Huber, "Organizational Learning: The Contributing Processes and the Literatures," *Organization Science*, February 1991.

Organizations are seen as learning by encoding inferences from history into routines that guide behavior.

Barbara Levitt and James G. March, "Organizational Learning," *American Review of Sociology,* Vol. 14, 1988.

Organizational learning is a process of detecting and correcting error.

Chris Argyris, "Double Loop Learning in Organizations," *Harvard Business Review,* September–October 1977.

Organizational learning occurs through shared insights, knowledge, and mental models . . . [and] builds on past knowledge and experience—that is, on memory.

Ray Stata, "Organizational Learning–The Key to Management Innovation," *Sloan Management Review,* Spring 1989.

Stages of Knowledge

SCHOLARS HAVE SUGGESTED that production and operating knowledge can be classified systematically by level or stage of understanding. At the lowest levels of manufacturing knowledge, little is known other than the characteristics of a good product. Production remains an art, and there are few clearly articulated standards or rules. An example would be Stradivarius violins. Experts agree that they produce vastly superior sound, but no one can specify precisely how they were manufactured because skilled artisans were responsible. By contrast, at the highest levels of manufacturing knowledge, all aspects of production are known and understood. All materials and processing variations are articulated and accounted for, with rules and procedures for every contingency. Here an example would be a "lights out," fully automated factory that operates for many hours without any human intervention.

In total, this framework specifies eight stages of knowledge. From lowest to highest, they are:

1. Recognizing prototypes (what is a good product?).

2. Recognizing attributes within prototypes (ability to define some conditions under which process gives good output).

3. Discriminating among attributes (which attributes are important? Experts may differ about relevance of patterns; new operators are often trained through apprenticeships).

4. Measuring attributes (some key attributes are measured; measures may be qualitative and relative).

5. Locally controlling attributes (repeatable performance; process designed by expert, but technicians can perform it).

6. Recognizing and discriminating between contingencies (production process can be mechanized and monitored manually).

7. Controlling contingencies (process can be automated).

8. Understanding procedures and controlling contingencies (process is completely understood).

Adapted from work by Ramchandran Jaikumar and Roger Bohn.[9]

Notes

1. Peter M. Senge, *The Fifth Discipline* (New York: Doubleday, 1990), p.1

2. Ikujiro Nonaka, "The Knowledge-Creating Company" *Harvard Business Review,* November–December 1991, p. 97.

3. Robert Howard, "The CEO as Organizational Architect: An Interview with Xerox's Paul Allaire," *Harvard Business Review*, September–October 1992, p. 106.

4. Modesto A. Maidique and Billie Jo Zirger, "The New Product Learning Cycle," *Research Policy*, Vol. 14, No. 6 (1985), pp. 299, 309.

5. Frank R. Gulliver, "Post-Project Appraisals Pay," *Harvard Business Review*, March–April 1987, p. 128.

6. David Nadler, "Even Failures Can Be Productive," *New York Times,* April 23, 1989, Sec. 3, p. 3.

7. Robert C. Camp, *Benchmarking: The Search for Industry Best Practices that Lead to Superior Performance* (Milwaukee: ASQC Quality Press, 1989), p. 12.

8. Roger Schank, with Peter Childers, *The Creative Attitude* (New York: Macmillan, 1988), p. 9.

9. Ramchandran Jaikumar and Roger Bohn, "The Development of Intelligent Systems for Industrial Use: A Conceptual Framework," *Research on Technological Innovation Management and Policy,* Vol. 3 (1986), pp. 182–188.

Originally published in July–August 1993
Reprint 93402

Teaching Smart People How to Learn

CHRIS ARGYRIS

Executive Summary

BEFORE A COMPANY can become a learning organization, it must first resolve a learning dilemma: competitive success increasingly depends on learning, but most people don't know how to learn. What's more, those members of the organization whom many assume to be the best at learning—professionals who occupy key leadership positions—are, in fact, not very good at it.

In this article, Harvard Business School professor Chris Argyris looks at human behavior patterns that block learning in organizations, explains why well-educated professionals are prone to these patterns, and tells how companies can improve the ability of their managers and employees to learn.

Effective learning is not a matter of the right attitudes or motivation. Rather, it is the product of the way people reason about their own behavior. When asked to exam-

81

ine their own role in an organization's problems, most people become defensive. They put the "blame" on someone else. This defensive reasoning keeps people from examining critically the way they contribute to the very problems they are committed to solving.

The solution: companies need to make the ways managers and employees reason about their behavior a key focus of organizational learning and continuous improvement programs. Teaching people how to reason about their behavior in new and more effective ways breaks down the defenses that block organizational learning.

Aɴʏ ᴄᴏᴍᴘᴀɴʏ ᴛʜᴀᴛ ᴀꜱᴘɪʀᴇꜱ to succeed in the tougher business environment of the 1990s must first resolve a basic dilemma: success in the marketplace increasingly depends on learning, yet most people don't know how to learn. What's more, those members of the organization that many assume to be the best at learning are, in fact, not very good at it. I am talking about the well-educated, high-powered, high-commitment professionals who occupy key leadership positions in the modern corporation.

Most companies not only have tremendous difficulty addressing this learning dilemma; they aren't even aware that it exists. The reason: they misunderstand what learning is and how to bring it about. As a result, they tend to make two mistakes in their efforts to become a learning organization.

First, most people define learning too narrowly as mere "problem solving," so they focus on identifying and correcting errors in the external environment. Solving problems is important. But if learning is to persist, managers and employees must also look inward. They need to reflect critically on their own behavior, identify the ways they often inadvertently contribute to the organization's problems, and then change how they act. In particular, they must learn how the very way they go about defining and solving problems can be a source of problems in its own right.

I have coined the terms "single loop" and "double loop" learning to capture this crucial distinction. To give a simple analogy: a thermostat that automatically turns on the heat whenever the temperature in a room drops below 68 degrees is a good example of single-loop learning. A thermostat that could ask, "Why am I set at 68 degrees?" and then explore whether or not some other temperature might more economically achieve the goal of heating the room would be engaging in double-loop learning.

Highly skilled professionals are frequently very good at single-loop learning. After all, they have spent much of their lives acquiring academic credentials, mastering one or a number of intellectual disciplines, and applying those disciplines to solve real-world problems. But ironically, this very fact helps explain why professionals are often so bad at double-loop learning.

Put simply, because many professionals are almost always successful at what they do, they rarely experience failure. And because they have rarely failed, they have never learned how to learn from failure. So whenever their single-loop learning strategies go wrong, they become defensive, screen out criticism, and put the "blame" on anyone and everyone but themselves. In short, their ability to learn shuts down precisely at the moment they need it the most.

The propensity among professionals to behave defensively helps shed light on the second mistake that companies make about learning. The common assumption is that getting people to learn is largely a matter of motivation. When people have the right attitudes and commitment, learning automatically follows. So companies focus on creating new organizational structures—compensation programs, performance reviews, corporate cultures, and the like—that are designed to create motivated and committed employees.

But effective double-loop learning is not simply a function of how people feel. It is a reflection of how they think—that is, the cognitive rules or reasoning they use to design and implement their actions. Think of these rules as a kind of "master program" stored in the brain, governing all behavior. Defensive reasoning can block learning even when the individual commitment to it is high, just as a computer program with hidden bugs can produce results exactly the opposite of what its designers had planned.

Companies can learn how to resolve the learning dilemma. What it takes is to make the ways managers and employees reason about their behavior a focus of organizational learning and continuous improvement programs. Teaching people how to reason about their behavior in new and more effective ways breaks down the defenses that block learning.

All of the examples that follow involve a particular kind of professional: fast-track consultants at major management consulting companies. But the implications of my argument go far beyond this specific occupational group. The fact is, more and more jobs—no matter what the title—are taking on the contours of "knowledge work." People at all levels of the organization must combine the mastery of some highly specialized technical expertise with the ability to work effectively in teams, form productive relationships with clients and customers, and critically reflect on and then change their own organizational practices. And the nuts and bolts of management—whether of high-powered consultants or service representatives, senior managers or factory technicians—increasingly consist of guiding and integrating the autonomous but interconnected work of highly skilled people.

How Professionals Avoid Learning

For 15 years, I have been conducting in-depth studies of management consultants. I decided to study consultants for a few simple reasons. First, they are the epitome of the highly educated professionals who play an increasingly central role in all organizations. Almost all of the consultants I've studied have MBAs from the top three or four U.S. business schools. They are also highly committed to their work. For instance, at one company, more than 90% of the consultants responded in a survey that they were "highly satisfied" with their jobs and with the company.

Professionals embody the learning dilemma: they are enthusiastic about continuous improvement—and often the biggest obstacle to its success.

I also assumed that such professional consultants would be good at learning. After all, the essence of their job is to teach others how to do things differently. I found, however, that these consultants embodied the learning dilemma. The most enthusiastic about continuous improvement in their own organizations, they were also often the biggest obstacle to its complete success.

As long as efforts at learning and change focused on external organizational factors—job redesign, compensation programs, performance reviews, and leadership training—the professionals were enthusiastic participants. Indeed, creating new systems and structures was precisely the kind of challenge that well-educated, highly motivated professionals thrived on.

And yet the moment the quest for continuous improvement turned to the professionals' own performance, something went wrong. It wasn't a matter of bad attitude. The professionals' commitment to excellence was genuine, and the vision of the company was clear. Nevertheless, continuous improvement did not persist. And the longer the continuous improvement efforts continued, the greater the likelihood that they would produce ever-diminishing returns.

What happened? The professionals began to feel embarrassed. They were threatened by the prospect of critically examining their own role in the organization. Indeed, because they were so well paid (and generally believed that their employers were supportive and fair), the idea that their performance might not be at its best made them feel guilty.

Far from being a catalyst for real change, such feelings caused most to react defensively. They projected the blame for any problems away from themselves and onto what they said were unclear goals, insensitive and unfair leaders, and stupid clients.

Consider this example. At a premier management consulting company, the manager of a case team called a meeting to examine the team's performance on a recent consulting project. The client was largely satisfied and had given the team relatively high marks, but the manager believed the team had not created the value added that it was capable of and that the consulting company had promised. In the spirit of continuous improvement, he felt that the team could do better. Indeed, so did some of the team members.

The manager knew how difficult it was for people to reflect critically on their own work performance, especially in the presence of their manager, so he took a number of steps to make possible a frank and open discussion. He invited to the meeting an outside consultant whom team members knew and trusted—"just to keep me honest," he said. He also agreed to have the entire meeting tape-recorded. That way, any subsequent confusions or disagreements about what went on at the meeting could be checked against the transcript. Finally, the manager opened the meeting by emphasizing that no subject was off limits—including his own behavior.

"I realize that you may believe you cannot confront me," the manager said. "But I encourage you to challenge me. You have a responsibility to tell me where you think the leadership made mistakes, just as I have the responsibility to identify any I believe you made. And all of us must acknowledge our own mistakes. If we do not have an open dialogue, we will not learn."

The professionals took the manager up on the first half of his invitation but quietly ignored the second. When asked to pinpoint the key problems in the experience with the client, they looked entirely outside themselves. The clients were uncooperative and arrogant. "They didn't think we could help them." The team's own managers were unavailable and poorly prepared. "At times, our managers were not up to speed before they walked into the client meetings." In effect, the professionals asserted that they were helpless to act differently—not because of any limitations of their own but because of the limitations of others.

The manager listened carefully to the team members and tried to respond to their criticisms. He talked about the mistakes that he had made during the consulting process. For example, one professional objected to the way the manager had run the project meetings. "I see that the way I asked questions closed down discussions," responded the manager. "I didn't mean to do that, but I can see how you might have believed that I had already made up my mind." Another team member complained that the manager had caved in to pressure from his superior to produce the project report far too quickly, considering the team's heavy work load. "I think that it was my responsibility to have said no," admitted the manager. "It was clear that we all had an immense amount of work."

Finally, after some three hours of discussion about his own behavior, the manager began to ask the team members if there were any errors *they* might have made. "After all," he said, "this client was not different from many others. How can we be more effective in the future?"

The professionals repeated that it was really the clients' and their own managers' fault. As one put it, "They have to be open to change and want to learn." The more the manager tried to get the team to examine its own responsibility for the outcome, the more the professionals bypassed his concerns. The best one team member could suggest was for the case team to "promise less"—implying that there was really no way for the group to improve its performance.

The case team members were reacting defensively to protect themselves, even though their manager was not acting in ways that an outsider would consider threatening. Even if there were some truth to their charges—the clients may well have been arrogant and closed, their own managers distant—the way they presented these claims was guaranteed to stop learning. With few exceptions, the professionals made attributions about the behavior of the clients and the managers but never publicly tested their claims. For instance, they said that the clients weren't motivated to learn but never really presented any evidence supporting that assertion. When their lack of concrete evidence was pointed out to them, they simply repeated their criticisms more vehemently.

If the professionals had felt so strongly about these issues, why had they never mentioned them during the project? According to the professionals, even this was the fault of others. "We didn't want to alienate the client," argued one. "We didn't want to be seen as whining," said another.

The professionals were using their criticisms of others to protect themselves from the potential embarrassment of having to admit that perhaps they too had contributed to the team's less-than-perfect performance. What's more, the fact that they kept repeating their defensive actions in the face of the manager's efforts to turn the group's attention to its own role shows that this defensiveness had become a reflexive routine. From the professionals' perspective, they weren't resisting; they were focusing on the "real" causes. Indeed, they were to be respected, if not congratulated, for working as well as they did under such difficult conditions.

The end result was an unproductive parallel conversation. Both the manager and the professionals were candid; they expressed their views forcefully. But they talked past each other, never finding a common language to describe what had happened with the client.

The professionals kept insisting that the fault lay with others. The manager kept trying, unsuccessfully, to get the professionals to see how they contributed to the state of affairs they were criticizing. The dialogue of this parallel conversation looks like this:

Professionals: "The clients have to be open. They must want to change."

Manager: "It's our task to help them see that change is in their interest."

Professionals: "But the clients didn't agree with our analyses."

Manager: "If they didn't think our ideas were right, how might we have convinced them?"

Professionals: "Maybe we need to have more meetings with the client."

Manager: "If we aren't adequately prepared and if the clients don't think we're credible, how will more meetings help?"

Professionals: "There should be better communication between case team members and management."

Manager: "I agree. But professionals should take the initiative to educate the manager about the problems they are experiencing."

Professionals: "Our leaders are unavailable and distant."

Manager: "How do you expect us to know that if you don't tell us?"

Conversations such as this one dramatically illustrate the learning dilemma. The problem with the professionals' claims is not that they are wrong but that they aren't useful. By constantly turning the focus away from their own behavior to that of others, the professionals bring learning to a grinding halt. The manager understands the trap but does not know how to get out of it. To learn how to do that requires going deeper into the dynamics of defensive reasoning—and into the special causes that make professionals so prone to it.

Defensive Reasoning and the Doom Loop

What explains the professionals' defensiveness? Not their attitudes about change or commitment to continuous improvement; they really wanted to work more effectively. Rather, the key factor is the way they reasoned about their behavior and that of others.

It is impossible to reason anew in every situation. If we had to think through all the possible responses every time someone asked, "How are you?" the world would pass us by. Therefore, everyone develops a theory of action—a set of rules that individuals use to design and implement their own behavior as well as to understand the behavior of others. Usually, these theories of actions become so taken for granted that people don't even realize they are using them.

One of the paradoxes of human behavior, however, is that the master program people actually use is rarely the one they think they use. Ask people in an interview or questionnaire to articulate the rules they use to govern their actions, and they will give you what I call their "espoused" theory of action. But observe these same people's behavior, and you will quickly see that this espoused theory has very little to do with how they actually behave. For example, the professionals on the case team said they believed in continuous improvement, and yet they consistently acted in ways that made improvement impossible.

When you observe people's behavior and try to come up with rules that would make sense of it, you discover a very different theory of action—what I call the individual's "theory-in-use." Put simply, people consistently act inconsistently, unaware of the contradiction between their espoused theory and their theory-in-use, between the way they think they are acting and the way they really act.

What's more, most theories-in-use rest on the same set of governing values. There seems to be a universal human tendency to design one's actions consistently according to four basic values:

1. To remain in unilateral control;

2. To maximize "winning" and minimize "losing";

3. To suppress negative feelings; and

4. To be as "rational" as possible—by which people mean defining clear objectives and evaluating their behavior in terms of whether or not they have achieved them.

The purpose of all these values is to avoid embarrassment or threat, feeling vulnerable or incompetent. In this respect, the master program that most people use is profoundly defensive. Defensive reasoning encourages individuals to keep private the premises, inferences, and conclusions that shape their behavior and to avoid testing them in a truly independent, objective fashion.

Because the attributions that go into defensive reasoning are never really tested, it is a closed loop, remarkably impervious to conflicting points of view. The inevitable response to the observation that somebody is reasoning defensively is yet more defensive reasoning. With the case team, for example, whenever anyone pointed out the professionals' defensive behavior to them, their initial reaction was to look for the cause in somebody else—clients who were so sensitive that they would have been alienated if the consultants had criticized them or a manager so weak that he couldn't have taken it had the consultants raised their concerns with him. In other words, the case team members once again denied their own responsibility by externalizing the problem and putting it on someone else.

The very success of professionals at education helps explain the problems they have with learning.

In such situations, the simple act of encouraging more open inquiry is often attacked by others as "intimidating." Those who do the attacking deal with their feelings about possibly being wrong by blaming the more open individual for arousing these feelings and upsetting them.

Needless to say, such a master program inevitably short-circuits learning. And for a number of reasons unique to their psychology, well-educated professionals are especially susceptible to this.

Nearly all the consultants I have studied have stellar academic records. Ironically, their very success at education helps explain the problems they have with learning. Before they enter the world of work, their lives are primarily full of successes, so they have rarely experienced the embarrassment and sense of threat that comes with failure. As a result, their defensive reasoning has rarely been activated. People who rarely experience failure, however, end up not knowing how to deal with it effectively. And this serves to reinforce the normal human tendency to reason defensively.

In a survey of several hundred young consultants at the organizations I have been studying, these professionals describe themselves as driven internally by an unrealistically high ideal of performance: "Pressure on the job is self-imposed." "I must not only do a good job; I must also be the best." "People around here are very bright and hardworking; they are highly motivated to do an outstanding job." "Most of us want not only to succeed but also to do so at maximum speed."

These consultants are always comparing themselves with the best around them and constantly trying to better their own performance. And yet they do not appreciate being required to compete openly with each other. They feel it is somehow inhumane. They prefer to be the individual contributor—what might be termed a "productive loner."

Behind this high aspiration for success is an equally high fear of failure and a propensity to feel shame and guilt when they do fail to meet their high standards. "You must avoid mistakes," said one. "I hate making them. Many of us fear failure, whether we admit it or not."

To the extent that these consultants have experienced success in their lives, they have not had to be concerned about failure and the attendant feelings of shame and guilt. But to exactly the same extent, they also have never developed the tolerance for feelings of failure or the skills to deal with these feelings. This in turn has led them not only to fear failure but also to fear the fear of failure itself. For they know that they will not cope with it superlatively—their usual level of aspiration.

The consultants use two intriguing metaphors to describe this phenomenon. They talk about the "doom loop" and "doom zoom." Often, consultants will perform well on the case team, but because they don't do the jobs perfectly or receive accolades from their managers, they go into a doom loop of despair. And they don't ease into the doom loop, they zoom into it.

As a result, many professionals have extremely "brittle" personalities. When suddenly faced with a situation

Performance evaluation is tailor-made to push professionals into the doom loop.

they cannot immediately handle, they tend to fall apart. They cover up their distress in front of the client. They talk about it constantly with their fellow case team members. Interestingly, these conversations commonly take the form of bad-mouthing clients.

Such brittleness leads to an inappropriately high sense of despondency or even despair when people don't achieve the high levels of performance they aspire to. Such despondency is rarely psychologically devastating, but when combined with defensive reasoning, it can result in a formidable predisposition against learning.

There is no better example of how this brittleness can disrupt an organization than performance evaluations. Because it represents the one moment when a professional must measure his or her own behavior against some formal standard, a performance evaluation is almost tailor-made to push a professional into the doom loop. Indeed, a poor evaluation can reverberate far beyond the particular individual involved to spark defensive reasoning throughout an entire organization.

At one consulting company, management established a new performance-evaluation process that was designed to make evaluations both more objective and more useful to those being evaluated. The consultants participated in the design of the new system and in general were enthusiastic because it corresponded to their espoused values of objectivity and fairness. A brief two years into the new process, however, it had become the object of dissatisfaction. The catalyst for this about-face was the first unsatisfactory rating.

Senior managers had identified six consultants whose performance they considered below standard. In keeping with the new evaluation process, they did all they could to communicate their concerns to the six and to help them improve. Managers met with each individual separately for as long and as often as the professional requested to explain the reasons behind the rating and to discuss what needed to be done to improve—but to no avail. Performance continued at the same low level and, eventually, the six were let go.

When word of the dismissal spread through the company, people responded with confusion and anxiety. After about a dozen consultants angrily complained to management, the CEO held two lengthy meetings where employees could air their concerns.

At the meetings, the professionals made a variety of claims. Some said the performance-evaluation process was unfair because judgments were subjective and biased and the criteria for minimum performance unclear. Others suspected that the real cause for the dismissals was economic and that the performance-evaluation procedure was just a fig leaf to hide the fact that the company was in trouble. Still others argued that the evaluation process was antilearning. If the company were truly a learning organization, as it claimed, then people performing below the minimum standard should be taught how to reach it. As one professional put it: "We were told that the company did not have an up-or-out policy. Up-or-out is inconsistent with learning. You misled us."

The CEO tried to explain the logic behind management's decision by grounding it in the facts of the case and by asking the professionals for any evidence that might contradict these facts.

Is there subjectivity and bias in the evaluation process? Yes, responded the CEO, but "we strive hard to reduce them. We are constantly trying to improve the process. If you have any ideas, please tell us. If you know of someone treated unfairly, please bring it up. If any of you feel that you have been treated unfairly, let's discuss it now or, if you wish, privately."

Is the level of minimum competence too vague? "We are working to define minimum competence more clearly," he answered. "In the case of the six, however, their performance was so poor that it wasn't difficult to reach a decision." Most of the six had received timely feedback about their problems. And in the two cases where people had not, the reason was that they had never taken the responsibility to seek out evaluations—and, indeed, had actively avoided them. "If you have any data to the contrary," the CEO added, "let's talk about it."

Were the six asked to leave for economic reasons? No, said the CEO. "We have more work than we can do, and letting professionals go is extremely costly for us. Do any of you have any information to the contrary?"

As to the company being antilearning, in fact, the entire evaluation process was designed to encourage learning. When a professional is performing below the minimum level, the CEO explained, "we jointly design remedial experiences with the individual. Then we look for signs of improvement. In these cases, either the professionals were reluctant to take on such assignments or they repeatedly failed when they did. Again, if you have information or evidence to the contrary, I'd like to hear about it."

The CEO concluded: "It's regrettable, but sometimes we make mistakes and hire the wrong people. If individuals don't produce and repeatedly prove themselves unable to improve, we don't know what else to do except dismiss them. It's just not fair to keep poorly performing individuals in the company. They earn an unfair share of the financial rewards."

Instead of responding with data of their own, the professionals simply repeated their accusations but in ways that consistently contradicted their claims. They said that a genuinely fair evaluation process would contain clear and documentable data about performance—but they were unable to provide firsthand examples of the unfairness that they implied colored the evaluation of the six dismissed employees. They argued that people shouldn't be judged by inferences unconnected to their actual performance—but they judged management in precisely this way. They insisted that management define clear, objective, and unambiguous performance standards—but they argued that any humane system would take into account that the performance of a professional cannot be precisely measured. Finally, they presented themselves as champions of learning—but they never proposed any criteria for assessing whether an individual might be unable to learn.

In short, the professionals seemed to hold management to a different level of performance than they held themselves. In their conversation at the meetings, they used many of the features of ineffective evaluation that they condemned—the absence of concrete data, for example, and the dependence on a circular logic of "heads we win, tails you lose." It is as if they were saying, "Here are the features of a fair performance-evaluation system. You should abide by them. But we don't have to when we are evaluating you."

Indeed, if we were to explain the professionals' behavior by articulating rules that would have to be in their heads in order for them to act the way they did, the rules would look something like this:

1. When criticizing the company, state your criticism in ways that you believe are valid—but also in ways that prevent others from deciding for themselves whether your claim to validity is correct.

2. When asked to illustrate your criticisms, don't include any data that others could use to decide for themselves whether the illustrations are valid.

3. State your conclusions in ways that disguise their logical implications. If others point out those implications to you, deny them.

Of course, when such rules were described to the professionals, they found them abhorrent. It was inconceivable that these rules might explain their actions. And yet in defending themselves against this observation, they almost always inadvertently confirmed the rules.

Learning How to Reason Productively

If defensive reasoning is as widespread as I believe, then focusing on an individual's attitudes or commitment is never enough to produce real change. And as the previous example illustrates, neither is creating new organizational structures or systems. The problem is that even when people are genuinely committed to improving their performance and management has changed its structures in order to encourage the "right" kind of behavior, people still remain locked in defensive reasoning. Either they remain unaware of this fact, or if they do become aware of it, they blame others.

There is, however, reason to believe that organizations can break out of this vicious circle. Despite the strength of defensive reasoning, people genuinely strive to produce what they intend. They value acting competently. Their self-esteem is intimately tied up with behaving consistently and performing effectively. Companies can use these universal human tendencies to teach people how to reason in a new way—in effect, to change the master programs in their heads and thus reshape their behavior.

People can be taught how to recognize the reasoning they use when they design and implement their actions. They can begin to identify the inconsistencies between their espoused and actual theories of action. They can face up to the fact that they unconsciously design and implement actions that they do not intend.

Until senior managers become aware of the ways they reason defensively, any change activity is likely to be just a fad.

Finally, people can learn how to identify what individuals and groups do to create organizational defenses and how these defenses contribute to an organization's problems.

Once companies embark on this learning process, they will discover that the kind of reasoning necessary to reduce and overcome organizational defenses is the same kind of "tough reasoning" that underlies the effective use of ideas in strategy, finance, marketing, manufacturing, and other management disciplines. Any sophisticated strategic analysis, for example, depends on collecting valid data, analyzing it carefully, and constantly testing the inferences drawn from the data. The toughest tests are reserved for the conclusions. Good strategists make sure that their conclusions can withstand all kinds of critical questioning.

So too with productive reasoning about human behavior. The standard of analysis is just as high. Human resource programs no longer need to be based on "soft" reasoning but should be as analytical and as data-driven as any other management discipline.

Of course, that is not the kind of reasoning the consultants used when they encountered problems that were embarrassing or threatening. The data they collected was hardly objective. The inferences they made rarely became explicit. The conclusions they reached were largely self-serving, impossible for others to test, and as a result, "self-sealing," impervious to change.

How can an organization begin to turn this situation around, to teach its members how to reason productively? The first step is for managers at the top to examine critically and change their own theories-in-use. Until senior managers become aware of how they reason defensively and the counterproductive consequences that result, there will be little real progress. Any change activity is likely to be just a fad.

Change has to start at the top because otherwise defensive senior managers are likely to disown any transformation in reasoning patterns coming from below. If professionals or middle managers begin to change the way they reason and act, such changes are likely to appear strange—if not actually dangerous—to those at the top. The result is an unstable situation where senior managers still believe that it is a sign of caring and sensitivity to bypass and cover up difficult issues, while their subordinates see the very same actions as defensive.

The key to any educational experience designed to teach senior managers how to reason productively is to connect the program to real business problems. The best demonstration of the usefulness of productive reasoning is for busy managers to see how it can make a direct difference in their own performance and in that of the organization. This will not happen overnight. Managers need plenty of opportunity to practice the new skills. But once they grasp the powerful impact that productive reasoning can have on actual performance, they will have a strong incentive to reason productively not just in a training session but in all their work relationships.

One simple approach I have used to get this process started is to have participants produce a kind of rudimentary case study. The subject is a real business problem that the manager either wants to deal with or has tried unsuccessfully to address in the past. Writing the actual case usually takes less than an hour. But then the case becomes the focal point of an extended analysis.

For example, a CEO at a large organizational-development consulting company was preoccupied with the problems caused by the intense competition among the various business functions represented by his four direct reports. Not only was he tired of having the problems dumped in his lap, but he was also worried about the impact the interfunctional conflicts were having on the organization's flexibility. He had even calculated that the money being spent to iron out disagreements amounted to hundreds of thousands of dollars every year. And the more fights there were, the more defensive people became, which only increased the costs to the organization.

In a paragraph or so, the CEO described a meeting he intended to have with his direct reports to address the problem. Next, he divided the paper in half, and on the right-hand side of the page, he wrote a scenario for the meeting—much like the script for a movie or play— describing what he would say and how his subordinates would likely respond. On the left-hand side of the page, he wrote down any thoughts and feelings that he would be likely to have during the meeting but that he wouldn't express for fear they would derail the discussion.

But instead of holding the meeting, the CEO analyzed this scenario *with* his direct reports. The case became the catalyst for a discussion in which the CEO learned several things about the way he acted with his management team.

He discovered that his four direct reports often perceived his conversations as counterproductive. In the guise of being "diplomatic," he would pretend that a consensus about the problem existed, when in fact none existed. The unintended result: instead of feeling reassured, his subordinates felt wary and tried to figure out "what is he *really* getting at."

The CEO also realized that the way he dealt with the competitiveness among department heads was completely contradictory. On the one hand, he kept urging them to "think of the organization as a whole." On the other, he kept calling for actions—department budget cuts, for example—that placed them directly in competition with each other.

Finally, the CEO discovered that many of the tacit evaluations and attributions he had listed turned out to be wrong. Since he had never expressed these assumptions, he had never found out just how wrong they were. What's more, he learned that much of what he thought he was hiding came through to his subordinates anyway—but with the added message that the boss was covering up.

The CEO's colleagues also learned about their own ineffective behavior. They learned by examining their own behavior as they tried to help the CEO analyze his case. They also learned by writing and analyzing cases of their own. They began to see that they too tended to bypass and cover up the real issues and that the CEO was often aware of it but did not say so. They too made inaccurate attributions and evaluations that they did not express. Moreover, the belief that they had to hide important ideas and feelings from the CEO and from each other in order not to upset anyone turned out to be mistaken. In the context of the case discussions, the entire senior management team was quite willing to discuss what had always been undiscussable.

Learning to reason productively can be emotional—even painful. But the payoff is great.

In effect, the case study exercise legitimizes talking about issues that people have never been able to address before. Such a discussion can be emotional—even painful. But for managers with the courage to persist, the payoff is great: management teams and entire organizations work more openly and more effectively and have greater options for behaving flexibly and adapting to particular situations.

When senior managers are trained in new reasoning skills, they can have a big impact on the performance of the entire organization—even when other employees are still reasoning defensively. The CEO who led the meetings on the performance-evaluation procedure was able to defuse dissatisfaction because he didn't respond to professionals' criticisms in kind but instead gave a clear presentation of relevant data. Indeed, most participants took the CEO's behavior to be a sign that the company really acted on the values of participation and employee involvement that it espoused.

Of course, the ideal is for all the members of an organization to learn how to reason productively. This has happened at the company where the case team meeting took place. Consultants and their managers are now able to confront some of the most difficult issues of the consultant-client relationship. To get a sense of the difference productive reasoning can make, imagine how the original conversation

To question someone else's reasoning is not a sign of mistrust but a valuable opportunity for learning.

between the manager and case team might have gone had everyone engaged in effective reasoning. (The following dialogue is based on actual sessions I have attended with other case teams at the same company since the training has been completed.)

First, the consultants would have demonstrated their commitment to continuous improvement by being willing to examine their own role in the difficulties that arose during the consulting project. No doubt they would have identified their managers and the clients as part of the problem, but they would have gone on to admit that they had contributed to it as well. More important, they would have agreed with the manager that as they explored the various roles of clients, managers, and professionals, they would make sure to test any evaluations or attributions they might make against the data. Each individual would have encouraged the others to question his or her reasoning. Indeed, they would have insisted on it. And in turn, everyone would have understood that act of questioning not as a sign of mistrust or an invasion of privacy but as a valuable opportunity for learning.

The conversation about the manager's unwillingness to say no might look something like this:

Professional #1: "One of the biggest problems I had with the way you managed this case was that you seemed to be unable to say no when either the client or your superior made unfair demands." [Gives an example.]

Professional #2: "I have another example to add. [Describes a second example.] But I'd also like to say that we never really told you how we felt about this. Behind your back we were bad-mouthing you—you know, 'he's being such a wimp'—but we never came right out and said it."

Manager: "It certainly would have been helpful if you had said something. Was there anything I said or did that gave you the idea that you had better not raise this with me?"

Professional #3: "Not really. I think we didn't want to sound like we were whining."

Manager: "Well, I certainly don't think you sound like you're whining. But two thoughts come to mind. If I understand you correctly, you were complaining, but the complaining about me and my inability to say no was covered up. Second, if we had discussed this, I might have gotten the data I needed to be able to say no."

Notice that when the second professional describes how the consultants had covered up their complaints, the manager doesn't criticize her. Rather, he rewards her for being open by responding in kind. He focuses on the ways that he too may have contributed to the cover-up. Reflecting undefensively about his own role in the problem then makes it possible for the professionals to talk about their fears of appearing to be whining. The manager then agrees with the professionals that they shouldn't become complainers. At the same time, he points out the counterproductive consequences of covering up their complaints.

Another unresolved issue in the case team meeting concerned the supposed arrogance of the clients. A more productive conversation about that problem might go like this:

Manager: "You said that the clients were arrogant and uncooperative. What did they say and do?"

Professional #1: "One asked me if I had ever met a payroll. Another asked how long I've been out of school."

Professional #2: "One even asked me how old I was!"

Professional #3: "That's nothing. The worst is when they say that all we do is interview people, write a report based on what they tell us, and then collect our fees."

Manager: "The fact that we tend to be so young is a real problem for many of our clients. They get very defensive about it. But I'd like to explore whether there is a way for them to freely express their views without our getting defensive. . . ."

"What troubled me about your original responses was that you assumed you were right in calling the clients stupid. One thing I've noticed about consultants—in this company and others—is that we tend to defend ourselves by bad-mouthing the client."

Professional #1: "Right. After all, if they are genuinely stupid, then it's obviously not our fault that they aren't getting it!"

Professional #2: "Of course, that stance is antilearning and overprotective. By assuming that they can't learn, we absolve ourselves from having to."

Professional #3: "And the more we all go along with the bad-mouthing, the more we reinforce each other's defensiveness."

Manager: "So what's the alternative? How can we encourage our clients to express their defensiveness and at the same time constructively build on it?"

Professional #1: "We all know that the real issue isn't our age; it's whether or not we are able to add value to the client's organization. They should judge us by what we produce. And if we aren't adding value, they should get rid of us—no matter how young or old we happen to be."

Manager: "Perhaps that is exactly what we should tell them."

In both these examples, the consultants and their manager are doing real work. They are learning about their own group dynamics and addressing some generic problems in client-consultant relationships. The insights they gain will allow them to act more effectively in the future—both as individuals and as a team. They are not just solving problems but developing a far deeper and more textured understanding of their role as members of the organization. They are laying the groundwork for continuous improvement that is truly continuous. They are learning how to learn.

Originally published in May–June 1991
Reprint 91301

Putting Your Company's Whole Brain to Work

DOROTHY LEONARD AND SUSAAN STRAUS

Executive Summary

INNOVATE OR FALL BEHIND: the competitive imperative
for virtually all businesses today is that simple. Responding to that command is difficult, however, because innovation takes place when different ideas, perceptions,
and ways of processing and judging information collide.
And it often requires collaboration among players who
see the world differently. As a result, the conflict that
should take place constructively among ideas all too
often ends up taking place unproductively among
people. Disputes become personal, and the creative
process breaks down.

The manager successful at fostering innovation figures out how to get different approaches to grate
against one another in a productive process the authors
call creative abrasion. The authors have worked with a
number of organizations over the years and have

observed many managers who know how to make creative abrasion work for them. Those managers understand that different people have different thinking styles:
analytical or intuitive, conceptual or experiential, social
or independent, logical or values driven. They deliberately design a full spectrum of approaches and perspectives into their organizations and understand that cognitively diverse people must respect other thinking styles.
They set ground rules for working together to discipline
the creative process. Above all, managers who want to
encourage innovation need to examine what they do to
promote or inhibit creative abrasion.

INNOVATE OR FALL BEHIND: the competitive
imperative for virtually all businesses today is that
simple. Achieving it is hard, however, because innovation takes place when different ideas, perceptions, and
ways of processing and judging information collide.
That, in turn, often requires collaboration among various players who see the world in inherently different
ways. As a result, the conflict that should take place
constructively among ideas all too often ends up taking place unproductively among people who do not
innately understand one another. Disputes become
personal, and the creative process breaks down.

Generally, managers have two responses to this phenomenon. On the one hand, managers who dislike conflict—or value only their own approach—actively avoid
the clash of ideas. They hire and reward people of a
particular stripe, usually people like themselves. Their
organizations fall victim to what we call the *comfortable clone syndrome:* coworkers share similar interests

and training; everyone thinks alike. Because all ideas pass through similar cognitive screens, only familiar ones survive. For example, a new-business development group formed entirely of employees with the same disciplinary background and set of experiences will assess every idea with an unvarying set of assumptions and analytical tools. Such a group will struggle to innovate, often in vain.

On the other hand, managers who value employees with a variety of thinking styles frequently don't understand how to manage them. They act as if locking a group of diverse individuals in the same room will necessarily result in a creative solution to a problem. They overlook the fact that people with different styles often don't understand or respect one another, and that such differences can fuel personal disagreements. The "detail guy" dismisses the "vision thing"; the "concept man" deplores endless analysis; and the individualist considers the demands of a team an utter waste of time. They simply can't work together without help.

The manager successful at fostering innovation figures out how to get different approaches to grate against one another in a productive process we call *creative abrasion*. Such a manager understands that different people have different thinking styles: analytical or intuitive, conceptual or experiential, social or independent, logical or values driven. She deliberately designs a full spectrum of approaches and perspectives into her organization—whether that organization is a team, a work group, or an entire company—and she understands that cognitively diverse people must respect the thinking styles of others. She sets ground rules for working together to discipline the creative process. Above all, the manager who wants to encourage innovation in her organization needs to examine what she does to promote or inhibit creative abrasion.

We have worked with a number of organizations over the years and have observed many managers who know how to make creative abrasion work for them. In order to create new ideas and products, such managers actively manage the process of bringing together a variety of people who think and act in potentially conflicting ways.

How We Think

What we call *cognitive differences* are varying approaches to perceiving and assimilating data, making decisions, solving problems, and relating to other people. These approaches are *preferences* (not to be confused with skills or abilities). For instance, you may prefer to approach problems intuitively but in fact may be better trained to approach them analytically. Preferences are not rigid: most people can draw on a mixture of approaches and do not live their lives within narrow cognitive boundaries. We often stretch outside the borders of our preferred operating modes if the conditions are right and the stakes are high enough. That said, we all tend to have one or two preferred habits of thought that influence our decision-making styles and our interactions with others—for good or for ill.

The most widely recognized cognitive distinction is between left-brained and right-brained ways of thinking. This categorization is more powerful metaphorically than it is accurate physiologically; not all the functions commonly associated with the left brain are located on the left side of the cortex and not all so-called right-brained functions are located on the right. Still, the simple description does usefully capture radically different ways of thinking. An analytical, logical, and sequential approach to problem framing and solving (left-brained thinking) clearly differs from an intuitive, values-based, and nonlinear one (right-brained thinking).

Cognitive preferences also reveal themselves in work styles and decision-making activities. Take collaboration as opposed to independence. Some people prefer to work together on solving problems, whereas others prefer to gather, absorb, and process information by themselves. Each type does its best work under different conditions. Or consider thinking as opposed to feeling. Some people evaluate evidence and make decisions through a structured, logical process, whereas others rely on their values and emotions to guide them to the appropriate action.

We all have preferred habits of thought that influence how we make decisions and interact with others.

The list goes on. Abstract thinkers, for instance, assimilate information from a variety of sources, such as books, reports, videos, and conversations. They prefer learning *about* something rather than experiencing it directly. Experiential people, in contrast, get information from interacting directly with people and things. Some people demand quick decisions no matter the issue, whereas others prefer to generate a lot of options no matter the urgency. One type focuses on details, whereas the other looks for the big picture: the relationships and patterns that the data form.

Not surprisingly, people tend to choose professions that reward their own combination of preferences. Their work experience, in turn, reinforces the original preferences and deepens the associated skills. Therefore, one sees very different problem-solving approaches among accountants, entrepreneurs, social workers, and artists. Proof to an engineer, for example, resides in the numbers. But show a page of numerical data to a playwright, and, more persuaded by his intuition, he may well toss it aside. Of course, assessing people's likely approaches to problem solving only by their discipline can be as misleading as using gender or ethnicity as a guide. Within any profession, there are always people whose thinking styles are at odds with the dominant approach.

The best way for managers to assess the thinking styles of the people they are responsible for is to use an established diagnostic instrument as an assessment tool. A well-tested tool is both more objective and more thorough than the impressions of even the most sensitive and observant of managers. Dozens of diagnostic tools and descriptive analyses of human personality have been developed to identify categories of cognitive approaches to problem solving and communication. All the instruments agree on the following basic points:

- Preferences are neither inherently good nor inherently bad. They are assets or liabilities depending on the situation. For example, politicians or CEOs who prefer to think out loud in public create expectations that they sometimes cannot meet; but the person who requires quiet reflection before acting can be a liability in a crisis.

- Distinguishing preferences emerge early in our lives, and strongly held ones tend to remain relatively stable through the years. Thus, for example, those of us who crave certainty are unlikely ever to have an equal love of ambiguity and paradox.

• We can learn to expand our repertoire of behaviors, to act outside our preferred styles. But that is difficult—like writing with the opposite hand.

• Understanding others' preferences helps people communicate and collaborate.

Managers who use instruments with the credibility of the Myers-Briggs Type Indicator (MBTI®) or the Herrmann Brain Dominance Instrument (HBDI) find that their employees accept the outcomes of the tests and use them to improve their processes and behaviors. (See "Identifying How We Think: The Myers-Briggs Type Indicator®" on page 131 and the "Herrmann Brain Dominance Instrument," on page 134.)

How We Act

All the assessment in the world means nothing unless new understanding brings different actions. Instruments such as the MBTI® and the HBDI will help you understand yourself and will help others understand themselves. The managerial challenge is to use the insights that these instruments offer to create new processes and encourage new behaviors that will help innovation efforts succeed.

UNDERSTAND YOURSELF

Start with yourself. When you identify your own style, you gain insight into the ways your preferences unconsciously shape your style of leadership and patterns of communication. You may be surprised to discover that your style can stifle the very creativity you seek from your employees. Consider the experiences of two managers of highly creative organizations. Each was at odds with his direct reports—but for very different reasons.

Jim Shaw, executive vice president of MTV Networks, is a left-brained guy in a right-brained organization. Said Shaw:

> *I have always characterized the creative, right-brained, visionary-type people here as dreamers. What I've realized is that when a dreamer expressed a vision, my gut reaction was to say, 'Well, if you want to do that, what you've got to do is A, then B, then you have to work out C, and because you've got no people and you've got no satellite uplink, you'll have to do D and E.' I've learned that saying that to a creative type is like throwing up on the dream. When I say that stuff too soon, the dreamer personalizes it as an attack. I've learned not to put all of the things that need to be done on the table initially. I can't just blurt it all out—it makes me look like a naysayer. What I've learned to do is to leak the information gradually, then the dreamer knows that I am meeting him halfway.*

Jerry Hirshberg, president of Nissan Design International, ran into precisely the opposite problem. Hirshberg discovered that some of his employees craved the very kind of structure that he personally abhorred. Before this epiphany, he inundated them with information and expected creativity in return. In short, he tried to manage his employees the way *he* would have wanted to be managed. Hirshberg found, however, that a few individuals reacted to every suggestion with a "yes, but. . . ." Initially, he interpreted such hesitancy as an anti-innovation bias. But he eventually realized that some of his employees preferred to have more time both to digest problems and to construct logical approaches to his intuitively derived ideas. Given a bit of extra time, they would return to the project with solid, helpful, and insightful plans for implementation. Ironically, it was their commitment to the success of the initiative that caused the employees to hesitate: they wanted the best possible result. Hirshberg recognized that their contributions were as critical as his own or those of any of the other "right-brainers" in the company.

Both Shaw and Hirshberg came to realize that their own cognitive preferences unconsciously shaped their leadership styles and communication patterns. In fact, their automatic reactions initially stifled the very creativity they sought from their employees. And note that it was just as important for the predominantly right-brained manager to recognize the contributions of the logicians as it was for the left-brained manager to acknowledge the organic approach of the visionaries. Except in theoretical models, creativity is not the exclusive province of one side or the other.

To innovate successfully, you must hire, work with, and promote people who are unlike you.

If you want an innovative organization, you need to hire, work with, and promote people who make you uncomfortable. You need to understand your own preferences so that you can complement your weaknesses and exploit your strengths. The biggest barrier to recognizing the contributions of people who are unlike you is your own ego. Suppose you are stalled on a difficult problem. To whom do you go for help? Usually to someone who is on the same wavelength or to someone whose opinion you respect. These people may give you soothing strokes, but they are unlikely to help spark a new idea. Suppose you were to take the problem instead to someone with whom you often find yourself at odds, someone who rarely validates your ideas or perspectives. It may take courage and tact to get constructive feedback, and the process may not be exactly pleasant. But that feedback will likely improve the quality of your solution. And when your adversary recovers from his amazement at your request, he may even get along with you better because the disagreement was clearly intellectual, not personal.

FORGET THE GOLDEN RULE

Don't treat people the way you want to be treated. Tailor communications to the receiver instead of the sender. In a cognitively diverse environment, a message sent is not necessarily a message received. Some people respond well to facts, figures, and statistics. Others prefer anecdotes. Still others digest graphic presentations most easily. Information must be delivered in the preferred "language" of the recipient if it is to be received at all.

For example, say you want to persuade an organization to adopt an open office layout. Arguments appealing to the analytical mind would rely on statistics from well-documented research conducted by objective experts that prove that open architecture enhances the effectiveness of communication. Arguments geared toward the action-oriented type would answer specific questions about implementation: How long will the office conversion take? Exactly what kind of furniture is needed? What are the implications for acoustics? Argu-

> *In a cognitively diverse environment, a message sent is not necessarily a message received.*

ments aimed at people-oriented individuals would focus on such questions as, How does an open office affect relationships? How would this setup affect morale? and Are people happy in this sort of setup? Arguments crafted for people with a future-oriented perspective would include graphics as well as artists' renderings of the proposed environment. In short, regardless of how you personally would prefer to deliver the message, you will be more persuasive and better understood if you formulate messages to appeal to the particular thinking style of your listener.

CREATE WHOLE-BRAINED TEAMS

Either over time or by initial design, company or group cultures can become dominated by one particular cognitive style. IBM, in the days when it was known as "Big Blue," presented a uniform face to the world; Digital Equipment prided itself on its engineering culture. Such homogeneity makes for efficient functioning—and limited approaches to problems or opportunities. Companies with strong cultures can indeed be very creative, but within predictable boundaries: say, clever marketing or imaginative engineering. When the market demands that such companies innovate in different ways, they have to learn new responses. Doing so requires adopting a variety of approaches to solving a problem—using not just the right brain or the left brain but the *whole* brain.

Consider the all-too-common error made by John, a rising star in a large, diversified instrument company: he forfeited an important career opportunity because he failed to see the need for a whole-brained team. Appointed manager of a new-product development group, John had a charter to bring in radically innovative ideas for products and services for launch in three to six years. "Surprise me," the CEO said.

Given a free hand in hiring, John lured in three of the brightest M.B.A.'s he could find. They immediately went to work conducting industry analyses and sorting through existing product possibilities, applying their recently acquired skills in financial analysis. To complete the team, John turned to the pile of résumés on his desk sent to him by human resources. All the applicants had especially strong quantitative skills, and a couple were engineers. John was pleased. Surely a group of such intelligent, well-trained, rigorous thinkers would be able to come up with some radical innovations for the company. Ignoring advice to hire some right-brained people to stimulate different ideas, he continued to populate his group with left-brained wizards. After 18 months, the team had rejected all the proposed new projects in the pipeline on the basis of well-argued and impressively documented financial and technical risk analysis. But the team's members had not come up with a single new idea. The CEO was neither surprised nor pleased, and the group was disbanded just short of its second anniversary.

In contrast, Bob, a successful entrepreneur embarking on his latest venture, resisted the strong temptation to tolerate only like-minded people. He knew from his prior ventures that his highly analytical style alienated some of his most creative people. Despite his unusual degree of self-awareness, Bob came within a hair's breadth of firing a strong and experienced manager: Wally, his director of human resources. According to Bob, after several months on board, Wally appeared to be "a quart and a half low." Why? Because he was inattentive in budget meetings and focused on what Bob perceived as trivia—day care, flextime, and benefits. Before taking action, however, Bob decided to look at the management team through the lens of thinking styles. He soon realized that Wally was exactly the kind of person he needed to help him grow his small company. Wally contributed a key element that was otherwise missing in the management team: a sensitivity to human needs that helped the company foresee and forestall problems with employees. So Bob learned to meet Wally halfway. Describing his success in learning to work with Wally, he told us, "You would have been proud of me. I started our meetings with five minutes of dogs, kids, and station wagons." Although the concern Wally demonstrated for the workers in the company did not eliminate union issues completely, it did minimize antagonism toward management and made disputes easier to resolve.

The list of whole-brained teams that continue to innovate successfully is long. At Xerox PARC, social scientists work alongside computer scientists. For instance, computer scientist Pavel Curtis, who is creating a virtual world in which people will meet and mingle, is working with an anthropologist who understands how communities form. As a result, Curtis's cyberspace meeting places have more human touches and are more welcoming than they would have been had they been designed only by scientists. Another example is the PARC PAIR (PARC Artist In Residence) program, which links computer scientists with artists so that each may influence the other's perceptions and representations of the world. At Interval Research, a California think tank dedicated to multimedia technologies, Director David Liddle invites leaders from various disciplines to visit for short "sab-

baticals." The purpose is to stimulate a cross-fertilization of ideas and approaches to solving problems. The
resulting exchanges have helped Interval Research create and spin off several highly innovative start-ups. And
Jerry Hirshberg applies the whole-brain principle to hiring practices at Nissan Design by bringing designers into
his organization in virtual pairs. That is, when he hires a
designer who glories in the freedom of pure color and
rhythm, he will next hire a very rational, Bauhaus-
trained designer who favors analysis and focuses on
function.

Complete homogeneity in an organization's cognitive approach can be very efficient. But as managers at
Xerox PARC, Interval Research, and Nissan Design have
learned, no matter how brilliant the group of individuals, their contributions to innovative problem solving
are enhanced by coming up against totally different perspectives.

LOOK FOR THE UGLY DUCKLING

Suppose you don't have the luxury of hiring new people
yet find your organization mired in a swamp of stale
thinking patterns. Consider the experience of the CEO of
the U.S. subsidiary of a tightly controlled and conservative European chemical company. Even though the company's business strategy had never worked well in the
United States, headquarters pushed the CEO to do more
of the same. He knew he needed to figure out a fresh
approach because the U.S. company was struggling to
compete in a rapidly changing marketplace. But his
direct reports were as uniformly left-brained as his superiors in Europe and were disinclined to work with him to
figure out new solutions.

Rather than give up, the CEO tested thinking preferences further down in the organization. He found the cognitive disparity that he needed in managers one layer below his direct reports—a small but dynamic set of individuals whose countercultural thinking patterns had constrained their advancement. In this company, people with right-brained preferences were seen as helpful but were not considered top management material. They were never promoted above a certain level.

The CEO changed that. He elevated three managers with right-brained proclivities to the roles of senior vice president and division head—lofty positions occupied until then exclusively by left-brained individuals. The new executives were strong supporters of the

Successful managers spend time getting members of diverse groups to acknowledge their differences.

CEO's intentions to innovate and worked with him to develop new approaches to the business. They understood that their communication strategy with headquarters would be critical to their success. They deliberately packaged their new ideas in a way that appealed to the cognitive framework of their European owner. Instead of lecturing about the need to change and try new ideas as they had in the past, the Americans presented their ideas as ways of solving problems. They supported their positions with well-researched quantitative data and with calculated anticipated cost savings and ROI—and described how similar approaches had succeeded elsewhere. They detailed the specific steps they would follow to succeed. Within two years, the U.S. subsidiary embarked on a major organizational redesign effort that included such radical notions as permitting outside competition for internal services. The quality of internal services soared—as did the number of innovations generated by the company in the United States.

MANAGE THE CREATIVE PROCESS

Abrasion is not creative unless managers make it so. Members of whole-brained teams don't naturally understand one another, and they can easily come to dislike one another. Successful managers of richly diverse groups spend time from the outset getting members to acknowledge their differences—often through a joint exploration of the results of a diagnostic analysis—and devise guidelines for working together before attempting to act on the problem at hand. Managers who find it awkward or difficult to lead their groups in identifying cognitive styles or in establishing guidelines can usually enlist the aid of someone who is trained in facilitation.

People often feel a bit foolish creating rules about how they will work together. Surely, the thinking goes, we are all adults and have years of experience in dealing with group dynamics. That, of course, is the problem. Everyone has practiced dysfunctional behavior for years. We learn to value politeness over truth at our mothers' knees. (Who hasn't mastered the art of the white lie by age 16?) We often discount an argument if it has an element of emotion or passion. We opt out if we feel ignored—people with unappreciated thinking styles learn to sit against the wall during meetings (the organizational back-of-the-bus). And we usually don't even notice those behaviors because they are so routine.

But the cost of allowing such behaviors to overtake a group is too high. Bob Meyers, senior vice president of interactive media at NBC, uses a sports analogy to make the point: "On a football team, for example, you have to use all kinds of people. Like the little, skinny guy who can only kick the ball. He may not even look as if he belongs on the team. This guy can't stand up to the refrigerator types that play in other positions. But as long as he does his job, he doesn't need to be big. He can just do what he does best. The catch is that the team needs to recognize what the little skinny guy can do—or they lose the benefit of his talent."

Managing the process of creative abrasion means making sure that everyone in the group is talking.

Managing the process of creative abrasion means making sure that everyone is at the front of the bus and talking. Some simple but powerful techniques can be helpful. First, clarify why you are working together by keeping the common goal in front of the group at all times. "If the goal is a real-world one with shared accountability and timetables attached," one manager observed, "then everyone understands the relevance of honoring one another's differences."

Second, make your operating guidelines explicit. Effective guidelines are always simple, clear, and concise. For example, one group set up the following principles about handling disagreements: "Anyone can disagree about anything with anyone, but no one can disagree without stating the reason" and "When someone states an objection, everyone else should listen to it, try to understand it, treat it as legitimate, and counter with their reasons if they don't agree with it." Some principles are as simple as "discuss taboo subjects," "verify assumptions," and "arrive on time with your homework done."

Third, set up an agenda ahead of time that explicitly provides enough time for both *divergent* discussion to uncover imaginative alternatives and *convergent* discussion to select an option and plan its implementation. Innovation requires both types of discussion, but people who excel at different types can, as one manager observed, "drive each other nuts." Another manager said, "If you ask people comfortable with ambiguity whether they prefer A or B, they will ask, 'How about C?'" Meanwhile, the people who crave closure will be squirming in their seats at the seemingly pointless discussion. Moreover, if one approach dominates, the unbalanced group process can risk producing an unacceptable or unfeasible new product, service, or change. Clearly allocating time to the two different types of discussion will contain the frustrations of both the decisive types, who are constantly looking at their watches wanting the decision to be made now, and the ambiguous types, who want to be sure that all possible avenues for creativity have been explored. Otherwise, the decisive members generally will pound the others into silence by invoking time pressures and scheduling. They will grab the first viable option rather than the best one. Or if the less decisive dominate, the group may never reach a conclusion. Innovation requires both divergent and convergent thinking, both brainstorming and action plans.

DEPERSONALIZE CONFLICT

Diverse cognitive preferences can cause tremendous tensions in any group, yet innovation requires the cross-fertilization of ideas. And because many new products are systems rather than stand-alone pieces, many business projects cannot proceed without the cooperation of

people who receive different messages from the same
words and make different observations about the same
incidents. The single most valuable contribution that
understanding different thinking and communication
styles brings to the process of innovation is taking the
sting out of intellectual disagreements that turn personal.

Consider the experience of the product manager of a
radically new product for a medical supplies company.
Facing a strict deadline of just 14 months to design and
deliver a new surgical instrument, the manager's team
needed to pull together fast. Design felt misled by marketing, however, and manufacturing couldn't understand design's delay in choosing between two mechanical hinges. The disagreements turned personal, starting
with "you always . . ." and ending with "irresponsible
ignorance." Two months into the project, the manager
began to wonder whether he should disband the team
and start over again. But he knew that his boss, the vice
president of marketing, would not agree to extend
the deadline. "I was desperate," he recalled. "I decided
to make one last attempt at getting them to work
together."

The manager decided to experiment with an offsite
gathering of his staff, including sessions diagnosing cognitive preferences. When they returned to work, the
team members used the new language they had learned
to label their differences in opinion and style. "At first,
using the terms was kind of a joke," the manager
recalled. "They'd say things like, 'Well, of course I want
the schedule right now. I'm a J!' Yet you could tell that
people were really seeing one another in a different light,
and they weren't getting angry." The team made its
deadline; perhaps even more important, several mem-

bers voluntarily joined forces to work on the next itera-
tion of the product. This willingness to work together
generated more value for the company than just "warm
fuzzies." Critical technical knowledge was preserved in
one small, colocated group—knowledge that would have
been scattered had project members dispersed to different product lines. Moreover, keeping part of the team
together resulted in a rapid development time for the
derivative product.

People who do not understand cognitive preferences
tend to personalize conflict or avoid it—or both. The
realization that another person's approach is not
wrongheaded and stubborn, but merely predictably different, diffuses anger. For example, at Viacom, a planning session involving two managers had ground to a
halt. One manager simply wouldn't buy into the idea
that the other was presenting. Suddenly, the presenter
slapped his head and said, "Oooohhh! I get it! You're
left-brained! Give me half an hour to switch gears, and
I'll be right back. Let me try this one more time." The
left-brained manager laughingly agreed—he understood the paradigm—and the meeting resumed with
the presenter armed with quantitative data and a
much more cohesive and logical presentation. Establishing that kind of effective two-way communication
led to a common understanding of the issues at hand
and, ultimately, a solution.

Understanding that someone views a problem differently does not mean you will agree. But an important
element in understanding thinking styles is recognizing
that no one style is inherently better than another. Each
style brings a uniquely valuable perspective to the
process of innovation, just as each style has some nega-
tives associated with it. Stereotypes of the cold-hearted

logician, the absent-minded, creative scientist, and the bleeding-heart liberal have some basis in reality. If people even partially internalize the inherent value of different perspectives, they will take disagreements less personally and will be better able to argue and reach a compromise or a consensus with less animosity. They will be open to the possibility that an alien view of the world might actually enhance their own. They will be better equipped to listen for the "a-ha" that occurs at the intersection of different planes of thought.

Caveat Emptor

Personality analysis of the type we describe is no more than a helpful tool, and it has many limitations. The diagnostic instruments measure only one aspect of personality: preferences in thinking styles and communication. They do not measure ability or intelligence, and they do not predict performance. Neither the MBTI® nor the HBDI measure other qualities that are critical to successful innovation such as courage, curiosity, integrity, empathy, or drive.

Preferences tend to be relatively stable, but life experiences can affect them. For example, repeated application of the MBTI® over a period of years has revealed a tendency for people to drift from a thinking style toward a feeling style when they have children. For the most part, however, studies done with both the MBTI® and the HBDI suggest that people retain their dominant preferences throughout a variety of work and social circumstances.

One critical warning label should be attached to any of these diagnostic instruments: only trained individuals should administer them. Not only can results be incorrectly interpreted (for instance, what are intended to be neutral descriptions of preferences might be labeled "right" or "wrong" behavior), but they can also be misused to invade people's privacy or to stereotype them. Of course, it is a human tendency to simplify in order to comprehend complexities; we stereotype people all the time on the basis of their language, dress, and behavior. Because these diagnostics have the weight of considerable psychological research behind them, however, they can be dangerous when misused. Without structured, reliable diagnoses, judgments are likely to be superficial and flawed. And without a substantial investment of time and resources, managers can't expect abrasion to be creative.

ONE OF THE PARADOXES of modern management is that, in the midst of technical and social change so pervasive and rapid that it seems out of pace with the rhythms of nature, human personality has not altered throughout recorded history. People have always had distinct preferences in their approaches to problem solving. Why then is it only now becoming so necessary for managers to understand those differences? Because today's complex products demand integrating the expertise of individuals who do not innately understand one another. Today's pace of change demands that these individuals quickly develop the ability to work together. If abrasion is not managed into creativity, it will constrict the constructive impulses of individuals and organizations alike. Rightly harnessed, the energy released by the intersection of different thought processes will propel innovation.

Identifying How We Think:
The Myers-Briggs Type Indicator

THE MYERS-BRIGGS TYPE INDICATOR (MBTI®) is the most widely used personality-assessment instrument in the world. Designed by a mother-and-daughter team, Isabel Myers and her mother Katherine Cook Briggs, the MBTI is based on the work of Carl Jung. Myers and Briggs developed the instrument during World War II on the hypothesis that an understanding of personality preferences might aid those civilians who were entering the workforce for the first time to find the right job for the war effort. The instrument conforms to standard testing conventions and, at last count in 1994, had been taken by more than two and a half million people around the world. The MBTI® is widely used in business, psychology, and education, as well as in career counseling.

The MBTI® uses four different pairs of attributes to create a matrix of 16 personality types:

- Extraversion Versus Introversion.[1] The first pair looks at where people prefer to focus their attention. These E/I descriptors focus on the source of someone's mental energy: extraverts draw energy from other people; introverts draw energy from themselves. Each finds the other's preferred operating conditions enervating.

- Sensing Versus "Intuition." The second pair identifies how one absorbs information. "Sensors" (S) gather data through their five senses, whereas "iNtuitives" (N) rely on less direct perceptions, such as patterns, relationships, and hunches. For example, when asked to describe the same painting, a group of S's might com-

The MBTI®

		Sensing Types (S)	
		Thinking (T)	**Feeling (F)**
Introverts (I)	**Judging (J)**	**ISTJ** Serious, quiet, earn success by concentration and thoroughness. Practical, orderly, matter-of-fact, logical, realistic, and dependable. Take responsibility.	**ISFJ** Quiet, friendly, responsible, and conscientious. Work devotedly to meet their obligations. Thorough, painstaking, accurate. Loyal, considerate.
	Perceiving (P)	**ISTP** Cool onlookers—quiet, reserved, and analytical. Usually interested in impersonal principles, how and why mechanical things work. Flashes of original humor.	**ISFP** Retiring, quietly friendly, sensitive, kind, modest about their abilities. Shun disagreements. Loyal followers. Often relaxed about getting things done.
Extraverts (E)	**Perceiving (P)**	**ESTP** Matter-of-fact, do not worry or hurry, enjoy whatever comes along. May be a bit blunt or insensitive. Best with real things that can be taken apart or put together.	**ESFP** Outgoing, easygoing, accepting, friendly, make things fun for others by their enjoyment. Like sports and making things. Find remembering facts easier than mastering theories.
	Judging (J)	**ESTJ** Practical, realistic, matter-of-fact, with a natural head for business or mechanics. Not interested in subjects they see no use for. Like to organize and run activities.	**ESFJ** Warm-hearted, talkative, popular, conscientious, born cooperators. Need harmony. Work best with encouragement. Little interest in abstract thinking or technical subjects.

Intuitive Types (N)			
Feeling (F)	**Thinking (T)**		
INFJ Succeed by perseverance, originality, and desire to do whatever is needed or wanted. Quietly forceful, conscientious, concerned for others. Respected for their firm principles.	**INTJ** Usually have original minds and great drive for their own ideas and purposes. Skeptical, critical, independent, determined, often stubborn.	Judging (J)	Introverts (I)
INFP Care about learning, ideas, language, and independent projects of their own. Tend to undertake too much, then somehow get it done. Friendly, but often too absorbed.	**INTP** Quiet, reserved, impersonal. Enjoy theoretical or scientific subjects. Usually interested mainly in ideas, little liking for parties or small talk. Sharply defined interests.	Perceiving (P)	
ENFP Warmly enthusiastic, high-spirited, ingenious, imaginative. Able to do almost anything that interests them. Quick with a solution and to help with a problem.	**ENTP** Quick, ingenious, good at many things. May argue either side of a question for fun. Resourceful in solving challenging problems, but may neglect routine assignments.	Perceiving (P)	Extraverts (E)
ENFJ Response and responsible. Generally feel real concern for what others think or want. Sociable, popular. Sensitive to praise and criticism.	**ENTJ** Hearty, frank, decisive, leaders. Usually good at anything that requires reasoning and intelligent talk. May sometimes be more positive than their experience in an area warrants.	Judging (J)	

ment on the brush strokes or the scar on the subject's
left cheek, whereas a group of N's might imagine
from the troubled look in the subject's eyes that he
lived in difficult times or suffered from depression.

- Thinking Versus Feeling. The third pair indicates how
one makes decisions once information is gathered.
Feeling types (F) use their emotional intelligence to
make decisions based on values—their internal sense
of right and wrong. Thinking types (T) tend to make
decisions based on logic and "objective" criteria—their
assessment of truth and falsehood.

- Judging Versus Perceiving. The fourth pair describes
how a person is oriented toward the outer world.
Judging types (J) have a high need for closure. They
reach conclusions quickly based on available data
and move on. Perceiving types (P) prefer to keep their
options open. They wait until they have gathered what
they consider to be enough information to decide. J's
crave certainty, and P's love ambiguity.

To read descriptions of the personality types identified
in the MBTI®, see the matrix.

The Herrmann Brain Dominance Instrument

NED HERRMANN CREATED and developed the Herrmann
Brain Dominance Instrument (HBDI) while he was a manager at General Electric. Starting his research with large
groups within GE, he expanded it over 20 years through
tens of thousands of surveys and has validated the data
with prominent psychometric research institutions, including
the Educational Testing Service.

The HBDI measures a person's preference both for
right-brained or left-brained thinking and for conceptual or

experiential thinking. These preferences often correspond to specific professions. Engineers, for example, consistently describe themselves as analytical, mathematical, and logical, placing them on the left end of the continuum. Artists, in contrast, describe themselves as emotional, spatial, and aesthetic, placing them on the right end of the continuum.

The charts below show how the different preferences combine into four distinct quadrants and how one can use the chart to analyze teams with different cognitive preferences:

Composite One: The Homogeneous Team

The chart above shows that everyone in the group approaches problems and challenges with the same emphasis on correctness. As engineers, the members of the team know how to do things correctly. Although the quality of their work is excellent, the members are difficult to work with. They have their own ways of doing things, and they reject variations from set standards. As a corporate function, the team has long enjoyed a captive audience in the company. Recently, members found themselves in trouble when the company restructured and other functions in the organization were allowed to outsource engineering.

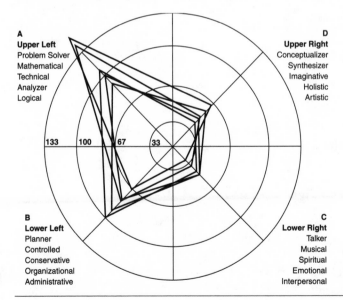

A	**D**
Upper Left	**Upper Right**
Problem Solver	Conceptualizer
Mathematical	Synthesizer
Technical	Imaginative
Analyzer	Holistic
Logical	Artistic

133   100   67   33

B	**C**
Lower Left	**Lower Right**
Planner	Talker
Controlled	Musical
Conservative	Spiritual
Organizational	Emotional
Administrative	Interpersonal

Composite Two: The Heterogeneous Team

The Management Services Group includes managers from information technology, the mail room, and the cafeteria. Although members share such goals as an orientation toward qualtiy, they encounter a wide range of business problems. The manager's dominant thinking style is in the lower right quadrant: a natural facilitator, she develops people, listens empathetically, and fosters a spirit of respect among her reports. Her leadership unified what had been a fragmented, inefficient collection of functions. Members regard one another as resources, enjoy the group's diversity, and take pride in their work.

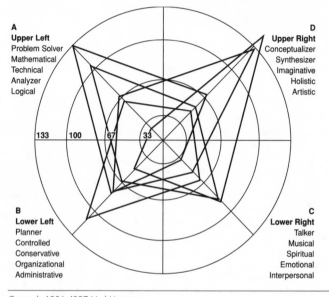

A
Upper Left
Problem Solver
Mathematical
Technical
Analyzer
Logical

D
Upper Right
Conceptualizer
Synthesizer
Imaginative
Holistic
Artistic

133 100 67 33

B
Lower Left
Planner
Controlled
Conservative
Organizational
Administrative

C
Lower Right
Talker
Musical
Spiritual
Emotional
Interpersonal

Note

1. MBTI® preferred spelling.

Originally published in July–August 1997
Reprint 97407

How to Make Experience Your Company's Best Teacher

ART KLEINER AND GEORGE ROTH

Executive Summary

IN OUR PERSONAL LIFE, experience is often the best teacher. Not so in corporate life. After a major event—a product failure, a downsizing crisis, or a merger—many companies stumble along, oblivious to the lessons of the past. Mistakes get repeated, but smart decisions do not. Most important, the old ways of thinking are never discussed, so they are still in place to spawn new mishaps.

Individuals will often tell you that they understand what went wrong (or right). Yet their insights are rarely shared openly. And they are analyzed and internalized by the company even less frequently. Why? Because managers have few tools with which to capture institutional experience, disseminate its lessons, and translate them into effective action.

In an effort to solve this problem, a group of social scientists, business managers, and journalists at MIT have developed and tested a tool called the learning history. It is a written narrative of a company's recent critical event, nearly all of it presented in two columns. In one column, relevant episodes are described by the people who took part in them, were affected by them, or observed them. In the other, learning historians—trained outsiders and knowledgeable insiders—identify recurrent themes in the narrative, pose questions, and raise "undiscussable" issues. The learning history forms the basis for group discussions, both for those involved in the event and for others who also might learn from it.

The authors believe that this tool—based on the ancient practice of community storytelling—can build trust, raise important issues, transfer knowledge from one part of a company to another, and help build a body of generalizable knowledge about management.

EXPERIENCE IS OFTEN THE BEST TEACHER—or so the saying goes. That is certainly true in our personal life. Why not, then, in corporate life? After a major event—a product failure, a wild business breakthrough, a downsizing crisis, or a merger—many companies seem to stumble along, oblivious to the lessons of the past. Mistakes get repeated, but smart decisions do not. Most important, the old ways of thinking that led to the mistakes are never discussed, which often means that they are still in place to spawn new mishaps again and again.

Ask individuals about those major events, however, and they often will tell you that they understand *exactly* what went wrong (or right). You might hear that the new product fizzled because no one in marketing listened to anyone in manufacturing—or vice versa. Or that the new product soared because the people in R&D or distribution "finally got their act together." Each point of view represents a valid, but limited, piece of the solution to the puzzle. If all these perspectives could be integrated coherently, the organization as a whole might learn what happened, why it happened, and what to do next.

Yet those insights are rarely shared openly. And they are analyzed, debated, and ultimately internalized by the whole organization even less frequently. In other words, in corporate life, even when experience is a good teacher, it's still only a private tutor. People in organizations act collectively, but they learn individually. That is the central tenet—and frustration—of organizational learning today.

The frustration exists because managers have few tools with which to capture institutional experience and disseminate its lessons. Employee surveys often are used to gather information and opinions about major events that have shaken up a business, but the assembled data rarely make it back to the organization's people in a form they can use meaningfully. "Best-practice" write-ups leave out the mistakes that people might learn from, as well as the hidden logic and struggles that have made breakthroughs possible. Sometimes consultants are called in to make sense of the "big something" that has happened, but their reports are rarely endorsed by those who experienced the event firsthand. The reports, after all, are aimed at the senior managers who hired the consultants. Once the consultants leave, the lessons of the past slip away with them, often to be sold to other companies.

A Different Approach to Institutional Learning

How, then, can organizations reflect collectively on past experience—and do so in such a way that people's thoughts and actions become more focused and energized? In other words, how can the lessons of the past be "processed" by an organization so that they are translated into more effective action?

Galvanized by those questions, a group of social scientists, business managers, and journalists at MIT's Center for Organizational Learning have spent the past four years developing and testing a tool to solve the conundrum of collective learning. We call our solution a *learning history*. (See "Creating a Learning History Piece by Piece," on pages 146–150.)

In the most basic terms, a learning history is a written narrative of a company's recent set of critical episodes: a corporate change event, a new initiative, a widespread innovation, a successful product launch, or even a traumatic event such as a major reduction in the work force. The document ranges in length from 20 to 100 pages, nearly all of it presented in two columns. In the right-hand column, relevant events are described by the people who took part in them, were affected by them, or observed them close-up. Managers, factory line workers, secretaries, and outsiders (such as customers, advertising copywriters, or suppliers) tell their part of the tale. Each person is quoted directly and identified only by title. The quotations are woven into an emotionally rich, cogent story reminiscent of Studs Terkel's unvarnished first-person accounts of American life and society.

The left-hand column is a different matter. It contains analysis and commentary by the *learning historians*. This small team is composed of trained outsiders, usually consultants and academics who specialize in organizational learning, as well as concerned and knowledgeable insiders, usually drawn from the company's human-resources department or organizational effectiveness staff. The team has sorted through hundreds of hours of interviews to distill the story in the right-hand column. In the process, it has come up with the text for the left-hand column, which identifies recurrent themes in the narrative, poses questions about its assumptions and implications, and raises "undiscussable" issues that hover just below the surface of the quotations to the right.

Once a learning history is complete, it is used as the basis for group discussions—for those involved in the event as well as for those who might learn from it. For instance, a learning history about one division's successful product rollout may be used to spark conversations in another division that is about to launch its own new product. The members of the second division are asked to read the

As in the old practice of community storytelling, people reexperience an event together and learn its meaning collectively.

learning history, marking portions of the text that excite, upset, or otherwise engage them. These people meet in small groups, holding in-depth conversations about the thought processes that led to the first group's success. The goal of the meetings is to gain a better understanding of the critical choices that the second group faces in planning new actions. Thus a learning history is as much a process as a product. (By contrast, traditional consulting reports are often distributed throughout an organization. Some are read; most are shelved.)

As for the product, its "jointly told tale" format may seem unique, but it is actually based on an ancient practice: community storytelling. Since the beginning of civilization, tribal peoples have gathered together, perhaps around a fire, to retell stories of important events: wars, changes in leadership, or natural disasters. During these gatherings, many individuals would offer their recollections (what we might call *perspectives*), and a shaman—the learning historian—would comment on the narrative, guiding a discovery process to bring the story's significance to light. The group would hear a multi-faceted tale with one directed purpose. Its members have thus reexperienced an event together and learned its meaning collectively. Indeed, the group has *created* this meaning together.

Are we suggesting that this timeless storytelling form will prove powerful in a corporate setting? Preliminary results indicate that the answer is yes. To date, more than 15 learning-history projects have been conducted, mainly at large U.S. companies trying to make sense of major, controversial incidents in their recent histories.

In one case, an auto manufacturer's product-launch team broke internal records for speed to market and quality; a subsequent learning history illuminated the new kinds of cross-functional interrelationships that had led to those results. In another case, a learning history examined the transformation effort at a *Fortune* 50 company, in which many entrenched business units had been eliminated, others had been combined, and several new ones had been introduced. Fallout from the transformation had left thousands of employees struggling with questions about the culture of the new organization and the role of managers within it. The learning history helped many people move forward by revealing the unspoken challenges with which the entire organization was wrestling—including how to act entrepreneurially in a company with a bureaucratic legacy.

Why Learning Histories Work

In general, we have observed that learning histories have several positive effects. First, and perhaps most important, they build trust. People who believe their opinions were ignored in the past come to feel that those opinions have been validated when they see them in the document (no matter who expressed them). People who have felt isolated come to believe they are not alone in their efforts to carve out a better future for themselves and the company. Finally, the group discussions that accompany the learning history provide new opportunities for collective reflection. They help people clear the air about their own concerns, fears, and assumptions, allowing them to develop a higher level of confidence in one another.

Learning histories raise issues that people want to talk about but have been afraid to discuss openly.

As trust grows, it creates an environment more conducive to learning—especially collective learning—because such learning depends on the candid sharing of ideas.

Second, learning histories seem particularly effective at raising issues that people would like to talk about but have not had the courage to discuss openly. The document, with its anonymous commentary from participants in the right-hand column and its pointed prompting in the left-hand column, provides the basis for more open conversations about difficult issues. In one learning history, a long-standing rivalry between two plants in a manufacturing company came to the surface in a way that demonstrated how both sides had, in effect, colluded to keep that rivalry going—at the expense of the quality of the machines they produced together.

Third, learning histories have proved successful at transferring knowledge from one part of a company to another. Instead of merely copying the lessons others have learned (which may not be appropriate for the new situation), readers of learning histories can discover the reasoning and impulses that led to those lessons, and apply the insights to the way they implement their own initiatives.

As an example of this phenomenon, consider the case of a learning history that was created for an oil refinery in the Midwest. For several years, the plant's managers and employees had sought better ways to control operating costs, to no avail. A breakthrough finally occurred when a cross-functional team decided to get to the bottom of a problem with an overheating compressor. In the course of discussing, planning, and executing a solution for the compressor, the team also developed a new maintenance strategy that helped solve a wide range of equipment problems at the refinery and ultimately saved $1.5 million. The purpose of the learning history about the breakthrough, however, was not to describe the technical solution per se. Instead, the 20-page document was distributed to the plant's 600 employees, and to a number of the company's refineries abroad, in order to demonstrate that innovative solutions could be forged internally.

"The learning history was extremely important to our proactive manufacturing effort," says one manager at the oil company. "It was a way for everyone—operators and managers alike—to recognize that a more proactive manufacturing approach had a shot, and maybe they should contribute to it. For the next two years, we referred back to the learning history at key moments. And we generated 50 more such innovations at the refinery."

Finally, learning histories help build a body of generalizable knowledge about management—about what works and what doesn't. Learning histories are commissioned to analyze one event, but their lessons often supersede it. For example, one recurring lesson is that "hard" results, such as financial returns or technical objectives, are frequently a function of "soft" issues, such as a company's culture. Indeed, the learning histories written to date have shown that in reengineering, redesign, or other change initiatives, the most critical factor for success is the quality of human interaction in the organization—which often depends on the humility and openness of the leaders who direct the effort. Learning histories contain other recurring themes as well—so many, in fact, that these documents may someday be routinely included among the textbooks and treatises in business schools and libraries, to be used as a source of insight for those engaged in developing the science of management.

The Future of Learning Histories

Without question, the learning history is emerging from its experimental stage. We will know more about this tool's effectiveness in several years' time, when we can revisit companies that have been through the process. Have the lessons of this newfangled document—rooted in an age-old tradition—continued to have an impact on those companies? Only experience will tell. After all, experience *can* be the best teacher, in both our individual and organizational lives.

Creating a Learning History Piece by Piece

The following excerpt is drawn from a 1996 learning history describing the successful launch of a car, disguised here with the name Epsilon, by a large automobile company, which we will call AutoCo. We originally were asked to create a learning history about the Epsilon project in order to help other vehicle-development teams within AutoCo learn from and improve on Epsilon's process and managerial innovations. For instance, Epsilon hit the market one week ahead of schedule, which is virtually unheard of in the car industry, and spent only $15 million of the $65 million budgeted for last-minute changes to the car's design. What had gone right? senior management wanted to know. And could the rest of the company experience the process vicariously, as it were?

For this particular document, the learning-history team consisted of the authors as well as three members of AutoCo's training and development group. We spent three months interviewing 45 people connected with the Epsilon project—from engineers to secretaries, and up the ladder through AutoCo management. We then spent three more months sifting through the thousands of pages of interview transcripts for meaningful, representative quotations; constructing the most relevant narrative story line; distilling central themes to be illuminated in the left-hand column; confirming all quotations with the original interviewees; and putting together the 89-page "book."

The following vignette was included in the learning history because it so aptly captured a central lesson of the Epsilon project. The car launch succeeded in large part because the Epsilon team continually broke and then reinvented AutoCo's rules and procedures. But this upending of business as usual also created conflict and confusion within the organization. Listen as those who lived through the experience tell their divergent versions of what happened.

The AutoCo learning history contained significant messages for the company. For example, if breaking AutoCo's rules was one reason why Epsilon succeeded, what was the function of those rules? Changing the rules would have other implications for everyone, from senior managers on down. For this reason, the learning history was not disseminated within the organization until senior managers had read, discussed, and accepted it. Indeed, a senior executive ended up writing the document's introduction, stating that managers recognized the importance of managing conflicting needs in large systems and that the document could help them learn to do so.

The learning history was subsequently discussed by hundreds of AutoCo employees in small groups, facilitated by internal consultants. It continues to be used by teams embarking on the challenging journey of product creation.

A → ## The Epsilon Project Is "Worse than Red!"

As they practiced their new management approach, the Epsilon product-launch team came to feel isolated from the rest of the AutoCo culture. They felt that senior managers sometimes applauded them, sometimes supported them, sometimes ignored them, and sometimes invalidated their efforts. Meanwhile, some senior leaders perceived the Ep-

B → silon team as withdrawing into their own "true believer" approach—as if Epsilon leaders felt that they knew how to achieve results that the rest of the AutoCo organization did not. This problem came to a head around *change requests* (CRs)—the engineering reports of issues, problems, and impending changes on a part—which reached a count of 524 at a time when a more typical car launch would have a high of 200.

Is it required that other groups share the perception of what a metric means and how it is used? What does this require of groups that seek to innovate processes?

Engineer: In the past, engineers would keep a hidden log of their problems. We would make them public only when we knew the answer. To say we were not rewarded for revealing CRs would be an understatement.

Typically, more than one person would be trying to solve the same problem. We would not know what each other was doing, because there was no common document that tracked the problem. I might be working to solve something involving sheet metal. The sheet metal people wouldn't know

C → because I didn't make it public on a CR out to the world. I might not even have known it affected sheet metal. When I finally wrote up my solution, they might say, "Wait a minute. We can't do this."

With our new process, we were encouraged to get CRs out into the open sooner. Now everyone knew each

The Epsilon Project Is "Worse than Red!" (continued)

other's problems in time to work together on a solution. This meant that the program manager had to empower us to handle our own problems.

Here a manager outside the Epsilon team expresses his dismay over the visible new signs of stress.

Senior manager: In manufacturing operations, we have a metric that starts with green and goes to yellow and goes to red. The Epsilon program was "purple," I said. That's worse than red! I've had a unique ability to say what's ready or not and be right 95% of the time. The Epsilon wasn't ready. The patient was terminal. I recommended postponing the launch date.

D → *What made it difficult for Epsilon managers to explain their strategy and behaviors in reporting of concerns?*

Epsilon team manager: Initially, I felt really good about our CR count. It was fantastic to find out about all these things and have them worked on. "By encouraging engineers to write concerns," I said to our vice president, "we're actually getting work done earlier and we'll have a better-quality product. This is a change in our system and we want to keep it that way. We want it to be not punitive for an engineer to write a concern early." [The vice president] nodded and listened. But after the meeting, he still said the program was out of control.

E —— *The vice president's perspective on the same incident is to the right. To him, the*

Vice president: The ethic that everybody was trying to follow was, There is a right time for change and there is a wrong time. Let us optimize the product and process so we have a quality

The Epsilon Project Is "Worse than Red!" (continued)

Epsilon project was not "out of control"; it was

F

simply going through the normal expansion and retraction of changes.

launch. That's the way it's supposed to work. It never does work that way. The engineers keep changing things, most of the time for good and relevant reasons. Manufacturing drives some changes. And so you have this constant battle of late failures, problems, fits, and finishes. There is huge pressure from manufacturing to drive the change count down.

One year later, under pressure over the high number of change requests, the program manager and the launch manager instituted a change in procedures. Engineers were told to stop everything else and resolve changes. During an intensive weekend, the engineers reduced the number of open CRs from 350 to 50. At the time, this enhanced the program's reputation. The program manager had demonstrated that he was

G

in firm control.

Ironically, however, the appearance of solving problems early may have contributed to an outbreak of late-breaking problems when changes that had been "pushed underground" resurfaced later in the game.

What sort of agreement or "buy-in" is it appropriate to ask for from other organizations and nonteam members ahead of time?

Engineer: But when management takes that approach, you drive your engineers underground. Nobody will write a CR that they don't have a solution for knowing that their supervisor has been told to come to them three times a week to ask them about open CRs. The engineer won't tell me about it. Thus, after we got through the VP build [the next-to-last prototype stage], it reverted back to the old "hidden" system.

The Epsilon Project Is "Worse than Red!" (continued)

In physics, there is a law specifying that any action is met by an equal and opposite reaction.

H ➤ *Does this law from the physical sciences also apply to the behavioral arena of managerial action? What would be your reaction to pressures to reduce CRs?*

Epsilon team manager: From then on, we tried to talk informally about our concerns. But that's not what you really want. You really want a formal system in place that lets everyone know when there is an issue. Once the whole company system knows a concern exists and it's a problem, they can all think about, "Now, how might that affect me?" Everybody can work on it together.

I even went back to [the vice president] and said, "The magic of this system is we capture everything. I mean everybody knows about it from the day we capture it." He thought that sounded terrific, but he still didn't like open concerns!

A.   Each short story within the learning history begins with a title meant to engage, or maybe even incite, the reader—just like the title of a novel or movie. We believe learning is a pull process, in which participants need to be drawn into an active intellectual role, as opposed to a push process, in which participants remain passive while lessons are pressed upon them.

B.   Each vignette begins with a full-column prologue, which sets the stage for the episode that follows. In this case, readers learn that Epsilon and AutoCo perpetually disagreed about *change requests* (CRs)—official reports issued by engineers alerting the system that changes in the car's design will be necessary. A learning history's prologue is invariably based on business outcomes or facts that no one would dispute. This signals to readers that the episode is worthy of their attention.

C.   In the right-hand column, participants (identified only by title or position) tell their part of the story. Quotations are selected because they move the story forward dramatically and represent

The Epsilon Project Is "Worse than Red!" (continued)

important perspectives on the episode. Here an engineer offers his version of events while revealing the assumptions and attitudes that made Epsilon engineers challenge the traditional CR protocol.

D.   The left-hand column provides commentary, insights, and questions brought forward by the learning historians. These comments are designed to provoke more reflective conversations when readers gather later in small groups to talk about the implications of the company's critical event.

E.   In this learning history, initial interviews were conducted with Epsilon team members. Because they talked about the reactions of AutoCo managers outside the project, it became necessary to interview some of those managers, such as this vice president, to make sure their points of view were included and treated fairly.

F.   This comment draws the reader's attention to the implicit meaning of the vice president's quotation; he was disagreeing with the Epsilon team's view but not saying so directly. Such unspoken disagreements are typical in any major change event. A learning history can bring these "silent" conflicts to the surface and make them rich fodder for discussion. In doing so, the learning history helps members of an organization understand, and often appreciate, why different perspectives exist.

G.   A full-column text interlude is used when a transition is needed. This text sets the context for later quotations as members of the organization continue to reflect—in this case, on the implications of the Epsilon team's compliant return to the "old system" for handling CRs.

H.   Learning histories can help companies make sense of a particular experience, but they are also designed to bring their readers up to 20,000 feet—to see that one experiences larger, generalizable lessons. Here a law of physics is stated to spark the insight that seemingly small changes can jolt the whole system.

Originally published in September–October 1997
Reprint 97506

Research That Reinvents
the Corporation

JOHN SEELY BROWN

Executive Summary

THE MOST IMPORTANT INVENTION that will come out of the corporate research lab in the future will be the corporation itself. As companies try to keep pace with rapid changes in technology and cope with unstable business environments, the research department has to do more than simply innovate new products. It must design the new technological and organizational "architectures" that make a continuously innovating company possible.

In this article, John Seely Brown, director of the Xerox Palo Alto Research Center (PARC), describes the business logic behind this distinctive vision of research's role and the ways PARC has tried to realize that vision. PARC researchers are prototyping new work practices as well as new technologies and products. They are designing new uses of technology to support the naturally occurring "local innovation" that takes place at all levels of any big company. And they are experimenting with new techniques for "coproducing" technological and organizational innovations—not only with other departments at Xerox but with the company's customers as well.

Xerox's business is technology, but Brown argues that any company, no matter what the business, must eventually grapple with the issues he raises. The successful company of the future must understand how people really work and how technology can help them work more effectively. It must know how to create an environment for continual innovation on the part of all employees. It must rethink traditional business assumptions and tap needs that customers don't even know they have yet. It must use research to reinvent the corporation.

THE MOST IMPORTANT INVENTION that will come out of the corporate research lab in the future will be the corporation itself. As companies try to keep pace with rapid changes in technology and cope with increasingly unstable business environments, the research department has to do more than simply innovate new products. It must design the new technological and organizational "architectures" that make possible a continuously innovating company. Put another way, corporate research must reinvent innovation.

At the Xerox Palo Alto Research Center (PARC), we've learned this lesson, at times, the hard way. Xerox created PARC in 1970 to pursue advanced research in computer science, electronics, and materials science. Over the next decade, PARC researchers were responsible for some of the basic innovations of the personal-computer revolution—only to see other companies commercialize these innovations more quickly than Xerox. (See "PARC: Seedbed of the Computer Revolution," on page 173.) In the process, Xerox gained a reputation for "fumbling the future," and PARC for doing brilliant research but in isolation from the company's business.

That view is one-sided because it ignores the way that PARC innovations *have* paid off over the past 20 years. Still, it raises fundamental questions that many companies besides Xerox have been struggling with in recent years: What is the role of corporate research in a business environment characterized by tougher competition and nonstop technological change? And how can large companies better assimilate the latest innovations and quickly incorporate them in new products?

One popular answer to these questions is to shift the focus of the research department away from radical breakthroughs toward incremental innovation, away from basic research toward applied research. At PARC, we have chosen a different approach, one that cuts across both of these categories and combines the most useful features of each. We call it pioneering research.

Like the best applied research, pioneering research is closely connected to the company's most pressing business problems. But like the best basic research, it seeks to redefine these problems fundamentally in order to come up with fresh—and sometimes radical—solutions. Our emphasis on pioneering research has led us to redefine what we mean by technology, by innovation, and indeed by research itself. (See "Letter to a Young Researcher," on page 175.) Here are some of the new principles that we have identified.

1. Research on new work practices is as important as research on new products.

Corporate research is traditionally viewed as the source of new technologies and products. At PARC, we believe it is equally important for research to invent new prototypes of organizational practice. This means going beyond the typical view of technology as an artifact—hardware and software—to explore its potential for creating new and more effective ways of working, what we call studying "technology in use." Such activities are essential for companies to exploit successfully the next great breakthrough in information technology: "ubiquitous computing," or the incorporation of information technology in a broad range of everyday objects.

2. Innovation is everywhere; the problem is learning from it.

When corporate research begins to focus on a company's practice as well as its products, another principle quickly becomes clear: innovation isn't the privileged activity of the research department. It goes on at all levels of a company—wherever employees confront problems, deal with unforeseen contingencies, or work their way around breakdowns in normal procedures. The problem is, few companies know how to learn from this local innovation and how to use it to improve their overall effectiveness. At PARC, we are studying this process of local innovation with employees on the front lines of Xerox's business and developing technologies to harvest its lessons for the company as a whole. By doing so, we hope to turn company size, so often seen as an obstacle to innovation, into an advantage—a rich seedbed of fresh insights about technology and new work practices.

3. Research can't just produce innovation; it must "coproduce" it.

Before a company can learn from the innovation in its midst, it must rethink the process by which innovation is transmitted throughout the organization. Research must "coproduce" new technologies and work practices by developing with partners throughout the organization a shared understanding of why these innovations are important. On the one hand, that means challenging the outmoded background assumptions that so often distort the way people see new technologies, new market opportunities, and the entire business. On the other, it requires creating new ways to communicate the significance of radical innovations. Essentially, corporate research must prototype new mental models of the organization and its business.

Innovation takes place at all levels of the company— not just in the research department.

4. *The research department's ultimate innovation partner is the customer.*

Prototyping technology in use, harvesting local innovation, coproducing new mental models of the organization—all these activities that we are pursuing inside Xerox are directly applicable to our customers as well. In fact, our future competitive advantage will depend not just on selling information-technology products *to* customers. It will depend on coproducing these products *with* customers—customizing technology and work practices to meet their current and future needs. One role of corporate research in this activity is to invent methods and tools to help customers identify their "latent" needs and improve their own capacity for continuous innovation.

At PARC, we've only begun to explore the implications of these new principles. Our activities in each of these areas are little more than interesting experiments. Still, we have defined a promising and exciting new direction. Without giving up our strong focus on state-of-the-art information technologies, we are also studying the human and organizational barriers to innovation. And using the entire Xerox organization of our laboratory, we are experimenting with new techniques for helping people grasp the revolutionary potential of new technologies and work practices.

The result: important contributions to Xerox's core products but also a distinctive approach to innovation with implications far beyond our company. Our business happens to be technology, but any company—no matter what the business—must eventually grapple with the issues we've been addressing. The successful company of the future must understand how people really work and how technology can help them work more effectively. It must know how to create an environment for continual innovation on the part of *all* employees. It must rethink traditional business assumptions and tap needs that customers don't even know they have yet. It must use research to reinvent the corporation.

Technology Gets Out of the Way

At the foundation of our new approach to research is a particular vision of technology. As the cost of computing power continues to plummet, two things become possible. First, more and more electronic technology will be incorporated in everyday office devices. Second, increased computing power will allow users to tailor the technology to meet their specific needs.

Both these trends lead to a paradoxical result. When information technology is everywhere and can be customized to match more closely the work to be done, the technology itself will become invisible. The next great breakthrough of the information age will be the disappearance of discrete information-technology products. Technology is finally becoming powerful enough to get out of the way.

Consider the photocopier. Ever since Chester Carlson first invented xerography some 50 years ago, the technology of photocopiers has been more or less the same. In a process somewhat similar to photography, a light-lens projects an image of the page onto a photoreceptor. The image is then developed with a dry toner to produce the copy. But information technology is transforming the copier with implications as radical as those accompanying the invention of xerography itself.

Today our copiers are complex computing and communications devices. Inside Xerox's high-end machines are some 30 microprocessors linked together by local area networks. They continually monitor the operations of the machine and make adjustments to compensate for wear and tear, thus increasing reliability and ensuring consistent, high as copy quality. Information systems inside our copiers also make the machines easier to use by constantly providing users with information linked to the specific task they are performing. (See "How Xerox Redesigned Its Copiers," on page 177.) These innovations were crucial to Xerox's success in meeting Japanese competition and regaining market share during the past decade.

But these changes are only the beginning. Once copiers become computing devices, they also become sensors that collect information about their own performance that can be used to improve service and product design. For example, Xerox recently introduced a new standard feature on our high-end copiers known as "remote interactive communication" or RIC. RIC is an expert system inside the copier that monitors the information technology controlling the machine and, using some artificial-intelligence techniques, predicts when the machine will next break down. Once RIC predicts a breakdown will occur, it automatically places a call to a branch office and downloads its prediction, along with its reasoning. A computer at the branch office does some further analysis and schedules a repair person to visit the site *before* the expected time of failure.

For the customer, RIC means never having to see the machine fail. For Xerox, it means not only providing better service but also having a new way to "listen" to our customer. As RIC collects information on the performance of our copiers—in real-world business environments, year in and year out—we will eventually be able to use that information to guide how we design future generations of copiers.

RIC is one example of how information technology invisible to the user is transforming the copier. But the ultimate conclusion of this technological transformation is the disappearance of the copier as a stand-alone device. Recently, Xerox introduced its most versatile office machine ever—a product that replaces traditional light-lens copying techniques with "digital copying," where documents are electronically scanned to create an image stored in a computer, then printed out whenever needed. In the future, digital copiers will allow the user to scan a document at one site and print it out somewhere else—much like a fax. And once it scans a document, a copier will be able to store, edit, or enhance the document—like a computer file—before printing it. When this happens, the traditional distinction between the copier and other office devices like computers, printers, and fax machines will disappear—leaving a flexible, multifunctional device able to serve a variety of user needs.

What is happening to the copier will eventually happen to all office devices. As computing power becomes ubiquitous—incorporated not only in copiers but also in filing cabinets, desktops, white boards, even electronic "post-it" notes—it will become more and more invisible, a taken-for-granted part of any work environment, much as books, reports, or other documents are today. What's more, increased computing power will make possible new uses of information technology that are far more flexible current systems. In effect, technology will become so flexible that users will be able to customize it ever-more precisely to meet their particular needs—a process that might be termed "mass customization." We are already beginning to see this development in software design. Increased computing power is making possible new approaches to writing software such as "object-oriented programming" (developed at PARC in the 1970s). This technique makes it easier for users to perform customizing tasks that previously required a trained programmer and allows them to adapt and redesign information systems as their needs change. From a purely technical perspective, object-oriented programming may be less efficient than traditional programming techniques. But the flexibility it makes possible is far more suited to the needs of constantly evolving organizations.

In the future, Xerox's chief product will be its customers' learning.

Indeed, at some point in the not-too-distant future—certainly within the next decade—information technology will become a kind of generic entity, almost like clay. And the "product" will not exist until it enters a specific situation, where vendor and customer will mold it to the work practices of the customer organization. When that happens, information technology as a distinct category of products will become invisible. It will dissolve into the work itself. And companies like ours might sell not products but rather the expertise to help users define their needs and create the products best suited to them. Our product will be our customers' learning.

Harvesting Local Innovation

The trend toward ubiquitous computing and mass customization is made possible by technology. The emphasis, however, is not on the technology itself but on the work practices it supports. In the future, organizations won't have to shape how they work to fit the narrow confines of an inflexible technology. Rather, they can begin to design information systems to support the way people really work.

That's why some of the most important research at PARC in the past decade has been done by anthropologists. PARC anthropologists have studied occupations and work practices throughout the company—clerks in an accounts-payable office who issue checks to suppliers, technical representatives who repair copying machines, designers who develop new products, even novice users of Xerox's copiers. This research has produced fundamental insights into the nature of innovation, organizational learning, and good product design.

We got involved in the anthropology of work for more than a good business reason. We figured that before we went ahead and applied technology to work,

we had better have a clear understanding of exactly how
people do their jobs. Most people assume—we did too,
at first—that the formal procedures defining a job or the
explicit structure of an organiza-
Some of our most   tional chart accurately describe
important research   what employees do, especially in
has been done by   highly routinized occupations.
anthropologists.   But when PARC anthropologist
Lucy Suchman began studying
Xerox accounting clerks in 1979, she uncovered an unexpected and intriguing contradiction.

When Suchman asked the clerks how they did their
jobs, their descriptions corresponded more or less to
the formal procedures of the job manual. But when she
observed them at work, she discovered that the clerks
weren't really following those procedures at all.
Instead, they relied on a rich variety of informal practices that weren't in any manual but turned out to be
crucial to getting the work done. In fact, the clerks
were constantly improvising, inventing new methods
to deal with unexpected difficulties and to solve immediate problems. Without being aware of it, they were
far more innovative and creative than anybody who
heard them describe their "routine" jobs ever would
have thought.

Suchman concluded that formal office procedures
have almost nothing to do with how people do their
jobs. People use procedures to understand the goals of a
particular job—for example, what kind of information a
particular file has to contain in order for a bill to be
paid—not to identify the steps to take in order to get
from here to there. But in order to reach that goal—
actually collecting and verifying the information and
making sure the bill is paid—people constantly invent

new work practices to cope with the unforeseen contingencies of the moment. These informal activities remain mostly invisible since they do not fall within the normal, specified procedures that employees are expected to follow or managers expect to see. But these "workarounds" enable an all-important flexibility that allows organizations to cope with the unexpected, as well as to profit from experience and to change.

If local innovation is as important and pervasive as we suspect, then big companies have the potential to be remarkably innovative—*if* they can somehow capture this innovation and learn from it. Unfortunately, it's the rare company that understands the importance of informal improvisation—let alone respects it as a legitimate business activity. In most cases, ideas generated by employees in the course of their work are lost to the organization as a whole. An individual might use them to make his or her job easier and perhaps even share them informally with a small group of colleagues. But such informal insights about work rarely spread beyond the local work group. And because most information systems now are based on the formal procedures of work, not the informal practices crucial to getting it done, they often tend to make things worse rather than better. As a result, this important source of organizational learning is either ignored or suppressed.

At PARC, we are trying to design new uses technology that leverage the incremental innovation coming from within the entire company. We want to create work environments where people can legitimately improvise, and where those improvisations can be captured and made part of the organization's collective knowledge base.

One way is to provide people with easy-to-use programming tools so they can customize the information
systems and computer applications that they work with.

Few companies understand the importance of informal improvisation, let alone respect it as a legitimate business activity.

To take a small example, my assistant is continu-
ally discovering new ways to improve the work systems in our office. She has more ideas for perfecting, say, our electronic calendar system than any researcher does.
After all, she uses it every day and frequently bumps up
against its limitations. So instead of designing a new and
better calendar system, we created a programming language known as CUSP (for "customized user-system
program") that allows users to modify the system themselves.

We've taken another small step in this direction at
EuroPARC, our European research lab in Cambridge,
England. Researchers there have invented an even more
advanced software system known as "Buttons"—bits of
computer code structured and packaged so that even
people without a lot of training in computers can modify
them. With Buttons, secretaries, clerks, technicians, and
others can create their own software applications, send
them to colleagues throughout the corporation over our
electronic mail network, and adapt any Buttons they
receive from others to their own needs. Through the use
of such tools, we are translating local innovation into
software that can be easily disseminated and used by all.

New technologies can also serve as powerful aids for
organizational learning. For example, in 1984 Xerox's
service organization asked us to research ways to

improve the effectiveness of their training programs. Training the company's 14,500 service technicians who repair copying machines is extremely costly and time-consuming. What's more, the time it takes to train the service work force on a new technology is key to how fast the company can launch new products.

The service organization was hoping we could make traditional classroom training happen faster, perhaps by creating some kind of expert system. But based on our evolving theory of work and innovation, we decided to take another approach. We sent out a former service technician, who had since gone on to do graduate work in anthropology, to find out reps actually do their jobs— not what they or their managers say they do but what they really do and how they learn the skills that they actually use. He took the company training program, actually worked of on repair jobs in the field, and inter-viewed tech-reps about their jobs. He concluded that the reps learn the most not from formal training courses but out in the field—by working on real problems and dis-cussing them informally with colleagues. Indeed, the sto-ries tech-reps tell each other—around the coffee pot, in the lunchroom, or while working together on a par-ticularly difficult problem—are crucial to continuous learning.

In a sense, these stories are the real "expert systems" used by tech-reps on the job. They are a storehouse of past problems and diagnoses, a template for construct-ing a theory about the current problem, and the basis for making an educated stab at a solution. By creating such stories and constantly refining them through conversa-tion with each other, tech-reps are creating a powerful "organizational memory" that is a valuable resource for the company.

As a result of this research, we are rethinking the design of tech-rep training—and the tech-rep job itself—in terms of lifelong learning. How might a company support and leverage the storytelling that is crucial to building the expertise not only of individual tech-reps but also of the entire tech-rep community? And is there any way to link that expertise to other groups in the company who would benefit from it—for example, the designers who are creating the future generations of our systems?

One possibility is to create advanced multimedia information systems that would make it easier for reps and other employees to plug in to this collective social mind. Such a system might allow the reps to pass around annotated video clips of useful stories, much like scientists distribute their scientific papers, to sites all over the world. By commenting on each other's experiences, reps could refine and disseminate new knowledge. This distributed collective memory, containing all the informal expertise and lore of the occupation, could help tech-reps—and the company—improve their capacity to learn from successes and failures.

Coproducing Innovation

Our approach to the issue of tech-rep training is a good example of what we mean by "pioneering" it; they actually acted it out in skits. They created research. We started with a real business problem, recognized by everyone, then reframed the problem to come up with solutions that no one had considered before. But this raises another challenge of pioneering research: How to communicate fresh insights about familiar problems so that others can grasp their significance?

The traditional approach to communicating new innovations—a process that usually goes by the name of "technology transfer"—is to treat it as a simple problem of transferring information. Research has to pour new knowledge into people's heads like water from a pitcher into a glass. That kind of communication might work for incremental innovations. But when it comes to pioneering research that fundamentally redefines a technology, product, work process, or business problem, this approach doesn't work.

It's never enough to just *tell* people about some new insight. Rather, you have to get them to experience it in a way that evokes its power and possibility. Instead of pouring knowledge into people's heads, you need to help them grind a new set of eyeglasses so they can see the world in a new way. That involves challenging the implicit assumptions that have shaped the way people in an organization have historically looked at things. It also requires creating new communication techniques that actually get people to experience the implications of a new innovation.

To get an idea of this process, consider the strategic implications of an innovation such as digital copying for a company like Xerox. Xerox owes its existence to a particular technology—light-lens xerography. That tradition has shaped how the company conceives of products, markets, and customer needs, often in ways that are not so easy to identify. But digital copying renders many of those assumptions obsolete. Therefore, making these assumptions explicit and analyzing their limitations is an essential strategic task.

Until recently, most people at Xerox thought of information technology mainly as a way to make traditional copiers cheaper and better. They didn't realize that digital copying would transform the business with broad implications not just for copiers but also for office information systems in general. Working with the Xerox corporate strategy office, we've tried to find a way to open up the corporate imagination—to get people to move beyond the standard ways they thought about copiers.

One approach we took a couple of years ago was to create a video for top management that we called the "unfinished document." In the video, researchers at PARC who knew the technology extremely well discussed the potential of digital copying to transform people's work. But they didn't just talk about mock-ups of the technology and then simulated how it might affect different work activities. They attempted to portray not just the technology but also the technology "in use."

We thought of the unfinished document as a "conceptual envisioning experiment"—an attempt to imagine how a technology might be used before we started building it. We showed the video to some top corporate officers to get their intuitional juices flowing. The document was "unfinished" in the sense that the whole point of the exercise was to get the viewers to complete the

One of our key research tasks is finding out how the company rejects new ideas.

video by suggesting their own ideas for how they might use the new technology and what these new uses might mean for the business. In the process, they weren't just learning about a new technology; they were creating a new mental model of the business.

Senior management is an important partner for research, but our experiments at coproduction aren't limited to the top. We are also involved in initiatives to get managers far down in the organization to reflect on the obstacles blocking innovation in the Xerox culture. For example, one project takes as its starting point the familiar fact that the best innovations are often the product of "renegades" on the periphery of the company. PARC researchers are part of a company group that is trying to understand why this is so often the case. We are studying some of the company's most adventuresome product-development programs to learn how the larger Xerox organization can sometimes obstruct a new product work process. By learning how the corporation rejects certain ideas, we hope to uncover those features of the corporate culture that need to change.

Such efforts are the beginning of what we hope will become an ongoing dialogue in the company about Xerox's organizational practice. By challenging the background assumptions that traditionally stifle innovation, we hope to create an environment where the creativity of talented people can flourish and "pull" new ideas into the business.

Innovating with the Customer

Finally, research's ultimate partner in coproduction is the customer. The logical end point of all the activities I have described is for corporate research to move outside the company and work with customers to coproduce the technology and work systems they will need in the future.

It is important to distinguish this activity from conventional market research. Most market research assumes either that a particular product already exists or that customers already know what they need. At PARC, we are focusing on systems that do not yet exist and on needs that are not yet clearly defined. We want to help customers become aware of their latent needs, then customize systems to meet them. Put another way, we are trying to prototype a need or use before we prototype a system.

One step in this direction is an initiative of Xerox's Corporate Research Group (of which PARC is a part) known as the Express project. Express is an experiment in product-delivery management designed to commercialize PARC technologies more rapidly by directly involving customers in the innovation process. The project brings together in a single organization based at PARC a small team of Xerox researchers, engineers, and marketers with employees from one of our customers— Syntex, a Palo Alto-based pharmaceutical company.

Syntex's more than 1,000 researchers do R&D on for their business, and progressively refine and tailor new drugs up for approval by the Food and Drug Administration. The Express team is exploring ways to use core technologies developed at PARC to help the pharmaceutical company manage the more than 300,000 "case report" forms it collects each year. (The forms report on tests of new drugs on human volunteers.) Syntex employees have spent time at PARC learning our technologies-in-progress. Similarly, the Xerox members of the team have intensively studied Syntex's work processes—much as PARC anthropologists have studied work inside our own company.

Once the project team defined the pharmaceutical company's key business needs and the PARC technologies that could be used to meet them, programmers from both companies worked together to create some prototypes. One new system, for example, is known as the Forms Receptionist. It combines technologies for document interchange and translation, document recognition, and intelligent scanning to scan, sort, file, and distribute Syntex's case reports. For Syntex, the new system solves an important business problem. For Xerox, it is the prototype of a product that we eventually hope to offer to the entire pharmaceutical industry.

We are also treating Express as a case study in coproduction, worth studying in its own right. The Express team has videotaped all the interactions between Xerox and Syntex employees and developed a computerized index to guide it through this visual database. And a second research team is doing an in-depth study of the entire Xerox-Syntex collaboration. By studying the project, we hope to learn valuable lessons about coproduction.

For example, one of the most interesting lessons we've learned from the Express project so far is just how long it takes to create a shared understanding among the members of such product teams—a common language, sense of purpose, and definition of goals. This is similar to the experience of many interfunctional teams that end up reproducing inside the team the same conflicting perspectives the teams were designed to overcome in the first place. We believe the persistence of such misunderstandings may be a serious drag on product development.

An "envisioning laboratory" could simulate the impact of a new product before it's actually built.

Thus a critical task for the future is to explore how information technology might be used to accelerate the creation of mutual understandings within work groups. The end point of this process would be to build what might be called an "envisioning laboratory"—a powerful computer environment where Xerox customers would have access to advanced programming tools for quickly modeling and envisioning the consequences of new systems. Working with Xerox's development and marketing organizations, customers could try out new system configurations, reflect on the appropriateness of the systems them to match their business needs. Such an environment would be a new kind of technological medium. Its purpose would be to create evocative simulations of new systems and new products before actually building them.

The envisioning laboratory does not yet exist. Still, it is not so farfetched to imagine a point in the near future where major corporations will have research centers with the technological capability of, say, a multimedia computer-animation studio like Lucas-film. Using state-of-the-art animation techniques, such a laboratory could create elaborate simulations of new products and use them to explore the implications of those products on a customer's work organization. Prototypes that today take years to create could be roughed out in a matter of weeks or days.

When this happens, phrases like "continuous innovation" and the "customer-driven" company will take on new meaning. And the transformation of corporate research—and the corporation as a whole—will be complete.

PARC: Seedbed of the Computer Revolution

FORMER XEROX CEO C. Peter McColough created the Palo Alto Research Center (PARC) in 1970 to perform basic research in computing and electronics and to study what McColough called "the architecture of information"—how complex organizations use information.

PARC hired some of the best computer scientists in the world and gave them virtually unlimited funding to pursue their ideas.

The scientific payoff from PARC was immediate. Throughout the 1970s, PARC researchers produced a series of fundamental innovations in computer technology that would prove to be the building blocks of the personal-computer revolution: "bit map" display computer screens that make easy-to-use graphic interfaces possible, local area networks for distributed computing, overlapping screen windows, point-and-click editing using a "mouse," and Smalltalk, the first object-oriented programming language.

Xerox never became a dominant player in the personal-computer industry. But PARC's research has nevertheless directly fed the company's strategic businesses. PARC developed the first prototype of laser printing in 1973. By 1990, laser printing was a several-billion-dollar business at Xerox. And PARC's innovations in local area networks and its distinctive computer interface designs have been successfully incorporated in Xerox copiers and printers, an innovation that was crucial to the company's successfully meeting the challenge from Japanese competition in the 1980s.

Where PARC scientists of the 1970s had a technical vision, today the center is increasingly focusing on the interrelationships between technology and work. In 1990, anthropologists, sociologists, linguists, and psychologists complement PARC's traditional research staff of computer scientists, physicists, and engineers. And much of the center's computer-science research emphasizes how information technology can be used to support effective group collaboration—a field known as computer-supported cooperative work.

—Robert Howard

XEROX

Xerox Corporation
Palo Alto Research Center
3333 Coyote Hill Road
Palo Alto, California 94304
415 494-4000

Letter to a Young Researcher

When we hire someone at PARC, there is one qualification we consider more important than technical expertise or intellectual brilliance: intuition. A well-honed intuition and the ability to trust it are essential tools for doing the kind of research we do here.

Our approach to research is "radical" in the sense conveyed by the word's original Greek meaning: "to the root." At PARC, we attempt to pose and answer basic questions that can lead to fundamental breakthroughs. Our competitive edge depends on our ability to invent radically new approaches to computing and its uses and then bring these rapidly to market.

This is different from what goes on at most corporate research centers, where the focus is on improving current technology and advancing the status quo. If you take a job somewhere else, when you embark on a project you will probably have a pretty good idea of how and when your work will pay off. The problems you address will be well defined. You will help to improve computer technology state of the art by going one step farther along a well-plotted path.

If you come to work here, there will be no plotted path. The problems you work on will be ones you help to invent. When you embark on a project, you will have to be prepared to go in directions you couldn't have predicted at the outset. You will be challenged to take risks and to give up cherished methods or beliefs in order to find new approaches. You will encounter periods of deep uncertainty and frustration when it will seem that your efforts are leading nowhere.

That's why following your instinct is so important. Only by having deep intuitions, being able to trust them, and knowing how to run with them will you be able to keep your bearings and guide yourself through uncharted territory. The ability to do research that gets to the root is what separates merely good researchers from world-class ones. The former are reacting to a predictable future; the latter are enacting a qualitatively new one.

Another characteristic we look for in our research staff is a commitment to solving real problems in the real world. Our focus is on technology *in use,* and people here are passionate about seeing their ideas embedded in products that shape the way people work, think, interact, and create.

At Xerox, both corporate executives and research scientists are strongly committed to making research pay off. Over the last few years, new channels of dialogue have opened between research and other parts of the company. In particular, corporate strategy and research shape and inform each other. PARC's strategic role will undoubtedly be further strengthened by the emergence of digital copying and the company's new focus on documents of all kinds, whether in digital or paper form. The fusion of two previously separate Xerox businesses—information systems and copying—means that the company will be able to capitalize on PARC's expertise in ways it has been unable to do in the past.

This is an exciting time to be embarking on a career in systems research. New tools and technologies make it possible to deliver large amounts of computing power to users, and this increase in power opens up possibilities for using computation in new ways.

If you come to work here, you will sacrifice the security of the safe approach in which you can count on arriving at a predictable goal. But you will have an opportunity to express your personal research "voice" and to help create a future that would not have existed without you.

Sincerely,

John Seely Brown
Corporate Vice President

Frank Squires
Vice President, Research Operations

How Xerox Redesigned Its Copiers

IN THE EARLY 1980S, Xerox's copier business faced a big problem. Service calls were increasing, and more and more customers were reporting that our newest copiers were "unreliable." The complaints couldn't have come at a worse time. We had been late to recognize market opportunities for low- and mid-range copiers, and Japanese competitors like Canon were cutting into our market share. Now Xerox's reputation for quality was at stake.

After interviewing some customers, we discovered that unreliability was not the real problem. Our copiers weren't breaking down more frequently than before; in fact, many of the service calls were unnecessary. But customers were finding the copiers increasingly difficult to use. Because they couldn't get their work done, they perceived the machines as unreliable.

The source of the problem was our copier design. Traditionally, Xerox technology designers—like most engineers—have strived to make machines "idiot proof." The idea was to foresee in advance all the possible things that could go wrong, then either design them out of the system or provide detailed instructions of what to do should they occur.

But as we kept adding new functions, we had to add more and more information, usually stored on flip cards attached to the machine. The copiers became so complex that it was harder for the new user to figure out how to do any particular task. To learn a new operation meant a time-consuming search through the flip cards. And whenever something went wrong—a paper jam, say, or a problem with the toner—the machines would flash a cryptic code number, which would require more flipping through the cards to find the corresponding explanation.

In many instances, users would encounter some obstacle, not be able to find out how to resolve it, and simply abandon the machine in mid-procedure. The next user to come along, unaware of the previous problem, would assume the machine was broken and call a repair person.

We had to make radical changes in copier design, but it was difficult to sell that message within the company. The idea that there might be serious usability problems with our machines met with resistance in the Xerox development organization that designs our copiers. After all, they had tested their designs against all the traditional "human factors" criteria. There was a tendency to assume that any problems with the machines must be the users' fault.

When researchers from PARC began to study the problem, we discovered that the human-factors tests used by the development group didn't accurately reflect how people actually used the machines. So a PARC anthropologist set up a video camera overlooking one of our new copiers in use at PARC, then had pairs of researchers (including some leading computer scientists) use the machine to do their own copying. The result was dramatic footage of some very smart people, anything but idiots, becoming increasingly frustrated and angry as they tried and failed to figure out how to get the machine to do what they wanted it to do.

The videos proved crucial in convincing the doubters that the company had a serious problem. Even more important, they helped us define what the real problem was. The videos demonstrated that when people use technology like a copier, they construct interpretations of it. In effect, they have a conversation with the machine much as two people have a conversation with each other. But our traditional idiot-proof design provided few cues to help the user interpret what was going on.

We proposed an alternative approach to design. Instead of trying to eliminate "trouble," we acknowledged that it was inevitable. So the copier's design should help users "manage" trouble—just as people manage and recover from misunderstandings during a conversation. This meant keeping the machine as transparent as possible by making it easy for the user to find out what is going on and to discover immediately what to do when something goes wrong.

Xerox's most recent copier families—the 10 and 50 series—reflect this new design principle. Gone are flip cards of earlier machines. Instead, we include enough computing power in the machines to provide customized

instructions on the display panel linked to particular procedures or functions. The information the user receives is
immediately put in the context of the task he or she is trying to perform. The new design also incorporates ideas
from PARC's research on graphical user interfaces for
computers. When something goes wrong, the display
panel immediately shows a picture of the machine that
visually indicates where the problem is and how to
resolve it.

The results of these changes have been dramatic.
Where it once took 28 minutes on average to clear a
paper jam, it takes 20 seconds with the new design. And
because such breakdowns are easier to fix, customers
are more tolerant of them when they occur.

Originally published in January–February 1991
Reprint 91101

Managing Professional Intellect

Making the Most of the Best

JAMES BRIAN QUINN,

PHILIP ANDERSON, AND

SYDNEY FINKELSTEIN

Executive Summary

A CORPORATION'S SUCCESS TODAY lies more in its
intellectual and systems capabilities than in its physical
assets. Managing human intellect—and converting it into
useful products and services—is fast becoming the critical
executive skill of the age. It is therefore surprising that so
little attention has been given to that endeavor.

This oversight is especially surprising because professional intellect creates most of the value in the new
economy, in service and manufacturing industries alike.
But few managers have systematic answers to even
these basic questions: What is professional intellect?
How can we develop it? How can we leverage it?

According to James Brian Quinn and his coauthors,
an organization's professional intellect operates on four
levels: cognitive knowledge, advanced skills, systems
understanding, and self-motivated creativity. They argue

that organizations that nurture self-motivated creativity are more likely to thrive in the face of today's rapid changes.

The authors offer best practices for developing professional intellect: recruiting the best people, forcing development and increasing challenges, and evaluating and weeding. And they illustrate how organizations as diverse as Merrill Lynch and NovaCare have leveraged professional intellect by linking new software tools, incentive systems, and organizational designs. The authors contend that organizations can tailor themselves to the particular way their professional intellect creates value by inverting the traditional hierarchical structure and by creating self-organizing networks.

IN THE POSTINDUSTRIAL ERA, the success of a corporation lies more in its intellectual and systems capabilities than in its physical assets. The capacity to manage human intellect—and to convert it into useful products and services—is fast becoming the critical executive skill of the age. As a result, there has been a flurry of interest in intellectual capital, creativity, innovation, and the learning organization, but surprisingly little attention has been given to managing professional intellect.

This oversight is especially surprising because professional intellect creates most of the value in the new economy. Its benefits are immediately visible in the large service industries, such as software, health care, financial services, communications, and consulting. But in manufacturing industries as well, professionals generate the preponderance of value—through activities like research and development, process design, product design, logistics, marketing, or systems management. Despite the growing importance of professional intellect, few managers have systematic answers to even these basic questions: What is professional intellect? How can we develop it? How can we leverage it?

What Is Professional Intellect?

The true professional commands a body of knowledge— a discipline that must be updated constantly. The professional intellect of an organization operates on four levels, presented here in order of increasing importance:

Cognitive knowledge (or know-what) is the basic mastery of a discipline that professionals achieve through extensive training and certification. This knowledge is essential, but usually far from sufficient, for commercial success.

Advanced skills (know-how) translate "book learning" into effective execution. The ability to apply the rules of a discipline to complex real-world problems is the most widespread value-creating professional skill level.

Systems understanding (know-why) is deep knowledge of the web of cause-and-effect relationships underlying a discipline. It permits professionals to move beyond the execution of tasks to solve larger and more complex problems—and to create extraordinary value. Professionals with know-why can anticipate subtle interactions and unintended consequences. The ultimate expression of systems understanding is highly trained intuition—for example, the insight of a seasoned research director who knows instinctively which projects to fund and exactly when to do so.

Self-motivated creativity (care-why) consists of will, motivation, and adaptability for success. Highly motivated and creative groups often outperform groups with greater physical or financial resources. Without self-motivated creativity, intellectual leaders can lose their knowledge advantage through complacency.

The value of intellect increases markedly as one moves up the scale from cognitive knowledge to self-motivated creativity.

They may fail to adapt aggressively to changing external conditions and particularly to innovations that obsolesce their earlier skills—just as the techniques of molecular design are superseding chemical screening in pharmaceuticals today. That is why the highest level of intellect is now so vital. Organizations that nurture care-why in their people can simultaneously thrive in the face of today's rapid changes and renew their cognitive knowledge, advanced skills, and systems understanding in order to compete in the next wave of advances.

Intellect clearly resides in the brains of professionals. The first three levels can also exist in the organization's systems, databases, or operating technologies, whereas the fourth is often found in its culture. The value of intellect increases markedly as one moves up the intellectual scale from cognitive knowledge to self-motivated creativity. Yet most enterprises focus virtually all their training attention on developing basic (rather than advanced) skills and little or none on systems or creative skills.

Most of a typical professional's activity is directed at perfection, not creativity. Customers primarily want professional knowledge delivered reliably and with the most advanced skill available. Although there is an occasional call for creativity, most of the work done by accounting units, hospitals, software companies, or financial service providers requires the repeated use of highly developed skills on relatively similar, though complex, problems. People rarely want surgeons, accountants, pilots, maintenance personnel, or nuclear plant operators to be very creative. Managers clearly must prepare their professionals for the few emergencies or other special circumstances that require creativity, but they should focus the bulk of their attention on delivering consistent, high-quality intellectual output.

Because professionals have specialized knowledge and have been trained as an elite, they often tend to regard their judgment in other realms as sacrosanct as well. Professionals generally hesitate to subordinate themselves to others or to support organizational goals not completely congruous with their special viewpoint. That is why most professional firms operate as partnerships and not as hierarchies, and why it is difficult for them to adopt a unified strategy.

Members of every profession tend to look to their peers to determine codes of behavior and acceptable standards of performance. They often refuse to accept evaluations by those outside their discipline. Many doctors, for example, resist the attempts of HMOs and insurance companies to tell them how to practice medicine. Such a posture is the source of many professional organizations' problems. Professionals tend to surround themselves with people who have similar backgrounds and values. Unless deliberately fractured, these discipline-based cocoons quickly become inward-looking bureaucracies that are resistant to change and detached from customers. Consider the many software or basic research organizations that become isolated inside larger organizations, creating conflicts with other professional groups such as marketing or manufacturing departments.

Developing Professional Intellect

At the heart of the most effective professional organizations we have observed are a handful of best practices for managing intellect that resemble successful coaching more than anything else.

Recruit the best. The leverage of intellect is so great that a few topflight professionals can create a successful organization or make a lesser one flourish. Marvin Bower essentially created McKinsey & Company; Robert Noyce and Gordon E. Moore spawned Intel; William H. Gates and Paul Allen built Microsoft; Herbert W. Boyer and Robert A. Swanson made Genentech; and Albert Einstein put Princeton's Institute for Advanced Study on the map. But even such organizations must find and attract extraordinary talent.

It is no accident that the leading management consultants devote enormous resources to recruiting and that they heavily screen the top graduates of the leading business schools. Microsoft interviews hundreds of highly recommended people for each key software designer it hires, and its grueling selection process tests not only cognitive knowledge but also the capacity to think about new problems under high pressure. The Four Seasons Hotels often interviews 50 candidates to make one hire. Venture capital firms, recognizing talent and commitment as the most critical elements for their success, spend as much time selecting and pursuing top people as they do making quantitative analyses of projects.

Because the most qualified professionals want to work with the best in their field, leading organizations can attract better talent than their lesser competitors. The best commercial programmers, for example, seek out and stay with Microsoft largely because they believe Microsoft will determine where the industry will move in the future and because they can share the excitement and rewards of being at that frontier. But second-tier organizations are not destined always to lag behind. Managers who understand the importance of the right kind of talent can pull a jujitsu reversal on industry leaders by acquiring such talent. When CEO Marshall N. Carter led State Street Bank's entry into the rapidly emerging custodials business, he hired world-class data processing managers to seed his new organization. Today State Street handles $1.7 trillion in custodial accounts, and virtually all its senior managers have data processing rather than traditional banking backgrounds.

Force intensive early development. Professional know-how is developed most rapidly through repeated exposure to the complexity of real problems. Thus for most professionals, the learning curve depends heavily on interactions with customers. Accordingly, the best companies systematically put new professionals in contact with customers, where they work under the watchful eye of an experienced coach. Microsoft, for example, assigns new software developers to small teams of three to seven people. Under the guidance of mentors, the developers participate in the design of complex new software systems at the frontier of users' needs.

The legendary 80-hour weeks and all-nighters that give investment bankers and software developers their bragging rights serve a more serious developmental purpose: They enable the best talent to move up a learning curve that is steeper than anyone else's. On-the-job training, mentoring, and peer pressure can force professionals to the top of their knowledge ziggurat. Although burnout can be a problem if people are pushed too far, many studies show that intensity and repetition are critical to developing advanced skills in fields as diverse as the law and piloting aircraft.

People who go through these intensive experiences become noticeably more capable and valuable—compared with their counterparts in less intensively managed organizations—within six months to a year. If they are properly coached, they also develop a greater in-depth feel for systems interactions (know-why) and identify more with the company and its goals

The best organizations push their professionals beyond the comfort of their book knowledge.

(care-why). The most successful organizations ensure such growth through constantly heightened (preferably customer-driven) complexity, thoroughly planned mentoring, substantial rewards for performance, and strong incentives to understand, systematize, and advance the discipline. The great intellectual organizations all seem to develop deeply ingrained cultures that emphasize these values. Most others do not.

Constantly increase professional challenges. Intellect grows most when professionals buy into a serious challenge. Leaders of the best organizations tend to be demanding, visionary, and intolerant of halfhearted efforts. They often set almost impossible "stretch goals"—as did Hewlett-Packard's William R. Hewlett (improve performance by 50%), Intel's Gordon Moore (double the number of components per chip each year), and Motorola's Robert W. Galvin (achieve six sigma quality). Some professionals may drop out in response to such demands. Others will substitute their own even higher standards. The best organizations constantly push their professionals beyond the comfort of their book knowledge, simulation models, and controlled laboratories. They relentlessly drive associates to deal with the more complex intellectual realms of live customers, real operating systems, and highly differentiated external environments and cultural differences. Mediocre organizations do not.

Evaluate and weed. Professionals like to be evaluated, to compete, to know they have excelled against their peers. But they want to be evaluated objectively and by people at the top of their field. Hence, heavy internal competition and frequent performance appraisal and feedback are common in outstanding organizations. As a result, there is a progressive winnowing of talent. For example, at Andersen Consulting, only 10% of the carefully selected professional recruits move on to partnerships—a process that takes 9 to 12 years. Microsoft tries to force out the lowest-performing 5% of its highly screened talent each year. Great organizations are unabashed meritocracies; great organizations that fail are often those that forget the importance of objective praise and selective weeding.

Leveraging Professional Intellect

Conventional wisdom has long held that there are few opportunities for leverage in professional activities. A pilot can handle only one aircraft at a time; a chef can cook only so many different dishes at once; a researcher can conduct only so many unique experiments; a doctor can diagnose only one patient's illness at a time. In such situations, adding professionals at the very least multiplies costs at the same rate as benefits. In the past, growth most often brought diseconomies of scale as the bureaucracies coordinating, monitoring, or supporting the professionals expanded faster than the professional base. Universities, hospitals, research firms, accounting groups, and consultancies all seemed to pay the price.

For years, there were only two ways in which many organizations could create leverage: by pushing their people through more intensive training or work schedules than their competitors or by increasing the number of "associates" supporting each professional. The latter practice even became the accepted meaning of the term *leverage* in the fields of law, accounting, and consulting.

But new technologies and management approaches are changing the traditional economics of managing professional intellect. Organizations as diverse as Merrill Lynch, Andersen Worldwide, and NovaCare have found effective ways to link new software tools, incentive systems, and organizational designs in order to leverage professional intellect to much higher levels. Although each organization has developed solutions tailored to the specific needs of its business, there are a handful of common underlying principles.

Boost professionals' problem-solving abilities by capturing knowledge in systems and software. The core intellectual competence of many financial organizations—such as Merrill Lynch and State Street Bank—lies in the human experts and the systems software that collect and analyze the data that are relevant to investment decisions. A few financial specialists working at headquarters leverage their own high-level analytical skills through close interactions with other specialists and "rocket scientist" modelers, and through access to massive amounts of data about transactions. Proprietary software models and databases leverage the intellect of those professionals, allowing them to analyze markets, securities, and economic trends in ways that otherwise would be beyond their reach. Software systems then distribute the resulting investment recommendations to brokers at retail outlets who create further value by customizing the center's advice in order to meet the needs of individual clients. If one thinks about this organization as a center connected to customers at multiple points of contact, or nodes, leverage equals the value of the knowledge multiplied by the number of nodes using it. Value creation is enhanced if experimentation at the center increases know-why and incentive structures stimulate care-why.

Merrill Lynch's retail brokerage business follows the basic structure outlined above. Roughly 18,000 Merrill Lynch brokers operate out of more than 500 geographically dispersed offices to create custom investment solutions for clients. The typical retail broker is not a highly skilled financial professional with years of advanced training. Yet the firm's brokers serve millions of clients worldwide with sophisticated investment advice and detailed, up-to-date information on thousands of complex financial instruments. Information systems make this extraordinary leverage possible.

Electronic systems capture Merrill Lynch's aggregate experience curve, quickly enabling less-trained people to achieve performance levels ordinarily associated with much more experienced personnel. The firm's computer network ensures that the retail brokers' cognitive knowledge is current and accurate. Merrill Lynch's information technologies allow the center to capture and distribute to the brokerage offices information about transactions, trading rules, yields, securities features, availability, tax considerations, and new offerings. Proprietary software, available on-line, serves as an instant training vehicle. It ensures that all brokers adhere to current regulations, make no arithmetic or clerical errors, and can provide customers with the latest market information. Capturing and distributing the firm's knowledge base through software allows Merrill Lynch to leverage the professional intellect at its core.

Information technology allows a large modern brokerage to be both efficient and flexible. At the center, it can achieve the full information power and economies of scale available only to a major enterprise. Yet local brokers can manage their own small units and accounts as independently as if they alone provided the service on a local basis. Their reward system is that of local entrepreneurs. The center functions primarily as an information source, a communications coordinator, or a reference desk for unusual inquiries. Field personnel connect with the center to obtain information to improve their performance, rather than to ask for instructions or specific guidance. At the same time, the center can electronically monitor local operations for quality and consistency. Most operating rules are programmed into the system and changed automatically by software. Electronic systems replace human command-and-control procedures. They also can eliminate most of the routine in jobs, free up employees for more personalized or skilled work, and allow tasks to be more decentralized, challenging, and rewarding.

Overcome professionals' reluctance to share information. Information sharing is critical because intellectual assets, unlike physical assets, increase in value with use. Properly stimulated, knowledge and intellect grow exponentially when shared. All learning and experience curves have this characteristic. A basic tenet of communication theory states that a network's potential benefits grow exponentially as the nodes it can successfully interconnect expand numerically. It is not difficult to see how this growth occurs. If two people exchange knowledge with each other, both gain information and experience linear growth. But if both then share their new knowledge with others—each of whom feeds back questions, amplifications, and modifications—the benefits become exponential. Companies that learn from outsiders—especially from customers, suppliers, and specialists such as advanced design or software firms—can reap even greater benefits. The strategic consequences of exploiting this exponential growth are profound. Once a company gains a knowledge-based competitive edge, it becomes ever easier for it to maintain its lead and ever harder for its competitors to catch up.

The tendency of each profession to regard itself as an elite with special values may get in the way of cross-disciplinary sharing.

Overcoming professionals' natural reluctance to share their most precious asset, knowledge, presents some common and difficult challenges. Competition among professionals often inhibits sharing, and assigning credit for intellectual contributions is difficult. When professionals are asked to collaborate as equals in problem solving, slow response is common as specialists try to refine their particular solutions to perfection. Because professionals' knowledge is their power base, strong inducements to share are necessary.

Even then, the tendency of each profession to regard itself as an elite with special cultural values may get in the way of cross-disciplinary sharing. Many professionals have little respect for those outside their field, even when all parties are supposedly seeking the same goal. Often, in manufacturing companies, researchers disdain product designers, who disdain engineers. In health care, basic researchers disdain physicians (because "they don't understand causation"). Physicians disdain both researchers (who "don't understand practical variations among real patients") and nurses (who "don't understand the discipline"). Nurses disdain both doctors and researchers (who "lack true compassion"). And all three groups disdain administrators (who are "nonproductive bureaucrats").

To facilitate sharing, Andersen Worldwide has developed an electronic system linking its 82,000 people operating in 360 offices in 76 countries. Known as ANet, the T1 and frame-relay network connects more than 85% of Andersen's professionals through data, voice, and video interlinks. ANet allows Andersen specialists—by posting problems on electronic bulletin boards and following up with visual and data contacts—to self-organize instantly around a customer's problem anywhere in the world. ANet thus taps into otherwise dormant capabilities and expands the energies and solution sets available to customers. Problem-solving capacity is further enhanced through centrally collected and carefully indexed subject, customer-reference, and resource files accessible directly through ANet or from CD-ROMs distributed to all offices.

Initially, Andersen spent large sums on hardware, travel, and professional training to encourage people not only to follow up on network exchanges but also to meet personally to discuss important problems—with disappointing results. Major changes in incentives and culture were needed to make the system work. Most important, participation in ANet began to be considered in all promotion and compensation reviews. To stimulate a cultural shift toward wider use of ANet, senior partners deliberately posed questions on employees' E-mail files each morning "to be answered by 10." Until those cultural changes were in place, ANet was less than successful despite its technological elegance.

Organize around intellect. In the past, most companies aimed to enhance returns from investments in physical assets: property, plant, and equipment. Command-and-control structures made sense when management's primary task was to leverage such physical assets. For example, the productivity of a manufacturing facility is determined largely by senior managers' decisions about capital equipment, adherence to standardized practices, the breadth of the product line, and capacity utilization. With intellectual assets, on the other hand, individual professionals typically provide customized solutions to an endless stream of new problems.

Inverting Organizations

Many successful enterprises we have studied have abandoned hierarchical structures, organizing themselves in patterns specifically tailored to the particular way their professional intellect creates value. Such reorganization often involves breaking away from traditional thinking about the role of the center as a directing force.

Consider NovaCare, the largest provider of rehabilitation care and one of the fastest-growing health-care companies in the United States. Its critical professional intellect resides in its more than 5,000 occupational, speech, and physical therapists. As professionals, they work alone to customize their expertise for individual patients at 2,090 locations in 40 states. To be of greatest value, they must be highly trained and constantly updated on the best practices in their fields.

By organizing around the work of its therapists, NovaCare achieves considerable leverage. To focus their time on serving patients' needs, the organization frees the therapists from administrative and business responsibilities by, for example, arranging and managing their contracts with care facilities, scheduling and reporting on treatments they give, handling their accounting and credit activities, providing them with training updates, and increasing their earnings through the company's marketing capabilities.

NovaCare's software system, NovaNet, captures and enhances much of the organization's systems knowledge, such as the rules with which therapists must comply and the information they need about customers, schedules, and billing; it highlights for executives those trends or problem areas most pertinent to future operations. NovaNet collects information from all therapists about, for example, their costs and services, techniques that have worked well, and changing care patterns in different regions. This information is vital for recruiting, training, motivating, and updating therapists.

To facilitate the collection and analysis of knowledge, NovaCare records its therapeutic care activities in ten-minute blocks. This detailed information creates a database that can be used by a diverse group of stakeholders: caregivers, hospitals, clinics, payers, government agencies, executives, and outside financial and regulatory bodies. NovaCare utilizes extensive peer and customer reviews in evaluating its therapists' work and (based on the time units captured in NovaNet) rewards them on the amount and quality of the care they deliver. NovaCare's professionals are highly self-sufficient; they have tremendous autonomy on questions involving patient care. Therapists can give orders to all intermediate line organizations. The company's regional and functional specialists in accounting, marketing, purchasing, and logistics exist primarily to support the therapists. Even CEO John H. Foster refers to the therapists as "my bosses." The leverage of NovaCare's organizational structure is "distributive"—that is, the support organization efficiently distributes logistics, analysis, and administrative support to the professionals. But it does not give them orders.

NovaCare has thus inverted the traditional organization. The former line hierarchy becomes a support structure, intervening only in extreme emergencies—as might the CEO of a hospital or the chief pilot of an airline. The function of former line managers changes: Instead of giving orders, they are now removing barriers, expediting resources, conducting studies, and acting as consultants. They support and help articulate the new culture. In effect, line managers evolve into staff people. (See the exhibit "In Inverted Organizations, Field Experts Become Bosses.")

Inverted organizations like NovaCare make sense when individual experts embody most of the organization's knowledge, when they do not have to interact with one another to solve problems, and when they customize their knowledge at the point of contact with customers. The software behind inverted systems must serve two somewhat conflicting goals: rules enforcement and professional empowerment. First, because professionals often resist regimentation, the software forces Nova-

Care's therapists to provide information in a consistent format, to comply with corporate rules and external regulations, and to originate the information necessary to monitor quality, costs, and trends for the organization's overall operation. Second, the software captures and distributes to professionals all the knowledge the company has built up over time so they can do their jobs better or more efficiently. That knowledge includes information about customers, professional databases, analytical models, successful solutions to problems, and access to specialized sources of knowledge.

Inverted organizations pose some unique managerial challenges. The apparent loss of formal authority can be traumatic for former line managers. And field people who are granted formal power may tend to act more and more like specialists with strictly "professional" outlooks

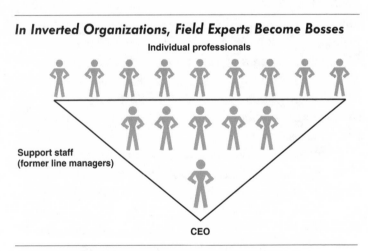

In Inverted Organizations, Field Experts Become Bosses

Individual professionals

Support staff
(former line managers)

CEO

The center provides support services that leverage the professionals in the field. Inverted organizations are appropriate when individual professionals have enough expertise to be self-sufficient and can act independently to meet specific customer needs. Many health-care providers, technical troubleshooting units, and universities are inverted organizations.

and to resist any set of organizational rules or business norms. Given those tendencies and without a disciplining software, field people often don't stay current with details about their organization's own complex internal systems. And their empowerment without adequate information and controls embedded in the company's technology systems can be dangerous. A classic example is the rapid decline of People Express, which consciously inverted its organization and enjoyed highly empowered and motivated point people but lacked the systems or the computer infrastructures to enable them to adapt as the organization grew.

If such organizations fail, it is usually because—despite much rhetoric about inversion—their senior managers did not support the concept with thoroughly overhauled performance-measurement and reward systems. Inverted systems rarely work until field people largely determine their "support people's" wages, promotions, and organizational progress. Former line people are reluctant to take this last crucial step. In our studies of more than 100 major structural changes in 60 large service organizations, less than 20% of the organizations had changed their performance-measurement systems significantly, and only about 5% had changed their reward systems (*Information Technology in the Service Society,* National Academy Press, 1993). Without such changes, the complications were predictable: People continued to perform according to the traditional measures.

Creating Intellectual Webs

In NovaCare's business, the professional therapists who create value are largely self-sufficient individual contributors. The inverted organization, coupled with the right software and incentives, allows NovaCare to enhance its therapists' productivity while giving them the operating autonomy they need. In other businesses, professional intellect is called on to create value by solving problems that exceed the capabilities of any solo practitioner. When problems become much more complex or less well defined, no one person or organization may know exactly what their full dimensions are, where key issues will ultimately reside, or who may have potential new solutions.

To tackle such problems—and to leverage their own intellectual assets to the maximum—a number of companies are using a form of self-organizing network that we call a *spider's web*. We use this term to avoid confusion with other, more traditional networklike forms more akin to holding companies or matrix organizations. Typically, a spider's web brings people together quickly to solve a particular problem and then disbands just as quickly once the job is done. The power of such interconnections is so great that even with a modest number of collaborating independent professionals (8 to 10), a spider's web can leverage knowledge capabilities by hundreds of times. (See the exhibit "In Spider's Webs, a Few Experts Team Up to Meet a Specific Challenge.")

Consider Merrill Lynch's mergers and acquisitions group. At the firm's center, specialists work primarily with others in their own disciplines—for example, acquisitions, high-yield financings, or equity markets. But when a large financing opportunity emerges, the project becomes an intellectual focal point and a team of specialists from different locations forms to pursue each individual deal. Such projects are so complex that, as one executive says,

At Merrill Lynch, people share knowledge because their compensation is attached to the mosaic of peer relationships.

"no one can be a know-everything banker. You can't have only specialists doing their own thing, and the client is not interested in dealing with multiple specialists." The key problem is focusing Merrill Lynch's rich but dispersed talents on a single customer's problem for a short time. Client-relationship managers, who best understand the customer's integrated needs, usually coordinate these teams, but they don't have direct, hierarchical control over team members.

Despite the current popularity of virtual organizations and of networks, few companies understand when and how to use networked forms to leverage professional intellect. As the Merrill Lynch example shows, networks can flexibly combine high specialization in

In Spider's Webs, a Few Experts Team Up to Meet a Specific Challenge

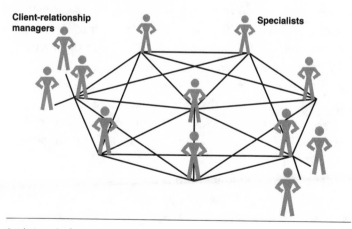

Client-relationship managers

Specialists

Spider's webs form to accomplish a particular project and disband when the project is completed. They are appropriate when knowledge is dispersed among many specialists, who must provide a coordinated solution to a complex customer problem. Many consulting firms, investment banks, research consortia, and medical diagnostic teams make use of spider's webs.

many different disciplines with multiple geographic contact points and a sharp focus on a single problem or customer set. But without the firm's specifically tailored promotion and compensation evaluation processes, the system probably would not work.

At Merrill Lynch, individuals work with many different colleagues on a variety of projects over the course of a year. All of them submit a confidential evaluation on everyone with whom they have worked closely. People are willing to share knowledge and cooperate because their compensation is attached to this mosaic of peer relationships, and compensation is a major motivating factor in this business. There are enough close personal team contacts to allow a truly mul-

How groups communicate is as important as the knowledge each center of excellence may have.

tifaceted picture of an individual's performance. According to one vice president of the mergers and acquisitions group, "In addition to profits generated, people are evaluated on how well they throw themselves into various projects, work with different groups to meet priorities, and meet clients' needs. The culture penalizes those who fail to be team players or to meet clients' needs. Under these rules, spider's webs have worked well in our relationship world. In our transactional world, however, we generally win by having the best specialists for that transaction."

Because each spider's web is unique in its purpose, patterns, and organizational power relationships, there is no single "best way" to manage all of them. For many projects, there may not be a single authority center. Often if the goal, problem, or solution is sufficiently clear, decisions may occur through informal processes if the parties agree. When the various centers of excellence need to operate in a highly coordinated fashion, they may delegate temporary authority to a project leader— as when widely dispersed researchers present a contract proposal. In other cases, the organization may designate one person as the lead in order to force decisions or to make final commitments—as when an insurance or investment banking consortium faces a deadline.

How groups communicate and what they voluntarily communicate are as important as the advanced knowledge each center of excellence may have. For virtually all purposes, however, encouraging shared interests, common values, and mutually satisfying solutions is essential for leveraging knowledge in these structures. Research suggests that to accomplish this goal, network managers should force members to overlap on different teams in order to increase continuity of contact, joint learning, and informal information sharing; purposely keep hierarchical relations ill defined; constantly update and reinforce project goals; avoid overly elaborate rules for allocating profits to individual nodes; develop continuous mechanisms for updating information about the external environment (for example, tax code changes, customer needs, or scientific results); involve both clients and peers in performance evaluations; and provide node members with both individual and team rewards for participation. Such consciously structured management interactions can mitigate the most common failures and frustrations.

The other key leverage factor in most spider's webs is technology. Electronics allow many more highly diverse, geographically dispersed, intellectually specialized talents to be brought to bear on a single project than ever before. Because public telecommunications networks allow interconnection almost anywhere, the key to effective network systems generally lies in software that provides a common language and database for communications, captures critical factual data about external environments, helps players find knowledge sources (usually through electronic menus, Web browsers like Netscape, or bulletin boards), and allows interactive sharing and problem solving. Each node will of course have its own specialized analytical software. But networking, groupware, and interactive software—along with a culture of and incentives for sharing—are the keys to success in these systems.

Much can be done to leverage professional intellect through extraordinary recruitment, training, and motivational measures. But, increasingly, managing human intellect alone is not enough. More radical organizational structures, supported by specifically designed software systems, are essential to capture, focus, and leverage capabilities to the fullest. Such systems have become the glue that both joins together highly dispersed service-delivery centers and leverages the critical knowledge bases, intellectual skills, and accumulated experience in professional organizations. They also bond professionals to the organization by providing them with databases, analytical models, and communication power that they cannot find elsewhere. These tools enable professionals to extend their performance beyond their personal limits, allowing them to achieve more inside the organization than they could on their own.

No organizational form is a panacea. In fact, many different forms often coexist successfully in the same company. Properly used, each helps a company attract, harness, leverage, and deploy intellect for a quite different purpose. Consequently, each requires a carefully developed set of cultural norms supported by software and by performance-measurement and reward systems tailored to the organization's specific purposes.

Originally published in March–April 1996
Reprint 96209

About the Contributors

PHILIP ANDERSON is an associate professor of business administration at the Amos Tuck School of Business Administration at Dartmouth College. On the editorial boards of four academic journals, he is also the editor of *Organization Science Electronic Letters*, the first department of a major academic business journal to be published via the Internet. He is the coauthor of *Managing Strategic Innovation and Change: A Collection of Readings and Inside the Kaisha: Demystifying Japanese Business Behavior* (HBS Press, 1997).

CHRIS ARGYRIS is the James Bryant Conant Professor of Education and Organizational Behavior at Harvard University. He has served as special consultant to the governments of England, France, Germany, Italy, and Sweden on problems of executive development and productivity. Professor Argyris is the author of three hundred articles and thirty books, including *Knowledge for Action: A Guide to Overlooking Barriers to Organizational Change and On Organizational Learning*. In 1994, Professor Argyris received the Academy of Management's Award for Lifetime Contributions to the Discipline of Management.

PETER F. DRUCKER is a writer, teacher, and consultant whose twenty-nine books have been published in more than twenty languages. He is the founder of the Peter F. Drucker Foundation for Nonprofit Management, and has counseled numerous governments, public service institutions, and major corporations. *Peter Drucker on the Profession of Management* (HBS Press, 1998) collects some of his best *Harvard Business Review* articles in one volume.

SYDNEY FINKELSTEIN is an associate professor of business administration at the Amos Tuck School of Business Administration at Dartmouth College, where he teaches courses on business policy and managing mergers and acquisitions. He is also the faculty director for Custom Executive Education Programs at Tuck, and a member of the faculty at Duxx Graduate School of Business Leadership in Monterrey, Mexico. An expert on mergers and acquisitions, and on managing knowledge flows in organizations, Professor Finkelstein currently serves on the editorial review boards of the *Strategic Management Journal, Administrative Science Quarterly, and Organization Science.* He is a consulting editor for the *Journal of Management,* and is the author of *Strategic Leadership: Top Executives and Their Effects on Organizations.*

DAVID A. GARVIN is the Robert and Jane Cizik Professor of Business Administration at the Harvard Business School. His research interests lie in the areas of general management and strategic change. He is the author most recently of the articles "The Processes of Organization and Management" (*Sloan Management Review,* 1998) and "Leveraging Processes for Strategic Advantage" (*Harvard Business Review,* 1995) and the videotape series *Working Smarter* (HBS Video, 1997) and

Putting the Learning Organization to Work (HBS Video, 1996).

ART KLEINER is the author of *The Age of Heretics*, a history of the corporate change movement after World War II, and a faculty member at New York University's Interactive Telecommunications Program. As president of Reflection Learning Associates, and coauthor and editorial director of *The Fifth Discipline Fieldbook*, he has been involved in the design and development of learning histories since their inception.

DOROTHY LEONARD holds the William J. Abernathy Professor of Business Administration chair at the Harvard Business School, where she has taught in MBA and executive education programs since 1983. She researches and consults in the areas of new technology commercialization, new product development, and the transfer of knowledge across geographic, cultural, and cognitive boundaries. She has published her work based on field research in more than two dozen articles in academic journals such as *Organization Science*. Her book *Wellspring of Knowledge* (HBS Press, 1995) describes and illustrates the managerial activities that sustain innovation and enhance strategic technological capabilities.

IKUJIRO NONAKA is the founding dean of the Graduate School of Knowledge Science at the Japan Advanced Institute of Science and Technology and a professor and former director of the Institute of Innovation Research at Hitotsubashi University, Tokyo. He is a senior editor of *Organization Science*, an international journal of the Institute of Management Science. In addition to authoring numerous articles, Professor Nonaka is the coauthor of *The Knowledge-Creating Company*, which was awarded the Best Book of the Year in Business and Management by the Association of American Publishers and Professional and Scholarly Publishing Division. He was recently named the first Xerox Distinguished Professor in Knowledge at the Haas School of Business, University of California, Berkeley.

JAMES BRIAN QUINN is the William and Josephine Buchanan Professor of Management, Emeritus, at the Amos Tuck School of Business Administration at Dartmouth. He is a recognized authority in the fields of strategic planning, the management of technological change, entrepreneurial innovation, and the impact of technology in the service sector. Professor Quinn has published extensively on both corporate and national policy issues involving strategic planning, research and development management, management of entrepreneurial organizations, and the impact of technology in services. His book *Intelligent Enterprise* won both the American Publisher's Association Award as Book of the Year in Business and Scholarship and the American Academy of Management's Book of the Year Award for Outstanding Contribution to Advancing Management Knowledge.

GEORGE ROTH is a researcher and lecturer at MIT's Sloan School of Management and executive director of the Ford/MIT Collaboration; a multi-million dollar alliance between MIT and Ford emphasizing learning, change, and knowledge-creation activities in engineering education, and research and environmental policy. His current research focuses on approaches to diffusing learning across organizations. A coauthor of the forthcoming second edition of *The Fifth Discipline Fieldbook*, Mr. Roth is presently studying and writing about companies' experiences in developing, sustaining, and transforming learning. Prior to his academic career, he spent ten years at Digital Equipment.

JOHN SEELY BROWN is the chief scientist of Xerox Corporation and the director of its Palo Alto Research Center (PARC). At Xerox, he has expanded the role of corporate research to include such topics as organizational learning, ethnographies of the workplace, complex adaptive systems, and techniques for unfreezing the corporate mind. His personal research interests include digital culture, ubiquitous computing, user-centering design, and organizational and individual learning. He has published more than sixty papers in scientific journals and received the *Harvard Business Review's* 1991 McKinsey Award for Research that Reinvents the Corporation. Dr. Brown edited *Seeing Differently: Insights on Innovation* (HBS Press, 1997).

SUSAAN STRAUS is a management consultant and internationally recognized speaker who specializes in organizational change and management team effectiveness. Her research with thousands of managers and executives in *Fortune* 500 companies has focused on the effect of cognitive preference and on the abilities of leaders, managers, and teams to face the challenges of innovating in a rapidly changing workplace. An experienced conflict mediator and process facilitator, she leads Performance Resources, whose mission is to elicit excellent performance in organizations committed to transformation and renewal.

Index

Knowledge is Power.
(So don't forget to recharge.)

For e-mail updates on powerful new business ideas and management issues, sign up for the *Harvard Business Review* listserv at **www.hbsp.harvard.edu.**

For ideas any time keep the Harvard Business School Publishing Web page in mind.

○ Access more than 7,500 articles, books, case studies, videos and CD-ROMs by leaders in management practice.
○ Search by author, key word, and more.
○ Order on-line and download *Harvard Business Review* articles any time.

Visit **www.hbsp.harvard.edu**, or call **(800) 668-6780** or **(617) 496-1449.**

 Harvard Business School Publishing
The power of ideas at work.